MAYER SMITH

The Oracle's Heart and the Cursed King

Contents

1	The Vision of Ruin	1
2	Summoned to the Throne	6
3	A Curse in Blood and Shadow	13
4	The Skeptical King	21
5	Echoes of a Forgotten Past	28
6	Whispers of Rebellion	36
7	A Bargain with Fate	45
8	The Touch of the Forbidden	52
9	The Oracle's Betrayal	59
10	A Kiss That Changes Destiny	65
11	The Assassin's Blade	72
12	The Rift Between Us	79
13	The Unraveling Curse	85
14	Betrayal in the Court	90
15	The Hidden Heir	96
16	A Heart Bound by Magic	102
17	The Battle for the Throne	108
18	The Oracle's Choice	116
19	The Death of Fate	122
20	A Love Beyond Destiny	128

One

The Vision of Ruin

The scent of burning incense curled through the air like the whisper of unseen spirits, filling the chamber with the cloying aroma of myrrh and sage. Elyra stood barefoot on the cold stone floor, her white robes pooling around her feet like mist. The torches flickered in their sconces, casting long, quivering shadows along the carved walls of the Oracle's Sanctuary. The flames danced as though they, too, feared what was about to unfold.

She was alone. She always was when the visions came.

Her pulse thrummed with the heaviness of knowing. Something was wrong tonight. A feeling had coiled deep in her chest ever since the last light of dusk faded from the sky. The omens had been restless, shifting in unnatural patterns, warning her that the tides of fate were turning.

Elyra lifted the ceremonial dagger from the stone altar before her. The blade was sharp, slender, and lined with ancient inscriptions—symbols that had existed long before men had learned to wield words. With a steady hand, she traced its cool metal against her palm, pressing just hard enough for the skin to break. A single drop of blood beaded at the surface, dark and glistening.

The moment the blood touched the altar, the chamber pulsed.

Elyra gasped as an invisible force yanked her forward, her body snapping rigid like a marionette caught in unseen strings. Her eyes rolled back, and her mind was no longer her own.

Darkness swallowed her.

Then, the vision came.

—-

She stood in the middle of a battlefield. The stench of death clung to the air, thick and suffocating. The sky was a violent shade of red, the sun dim behind a shroud of black clouds. The earth beneath her feet was slick with blood. Bodies lay strewn across the field, soldiers clad in royal armor, their lifeless eyes staring into the heavens.

And at the center of it all—he stood.

King Rhyven.

The ruler of Kharoth. The man whose fate had been written in the stars long before he was born.

His once-glorious armor was tarnished with gore, his black cloak tattered and drenched in the blood of friend and foe alike. He clutched a sword in his hand, the blade trembling as he struggled to remain standing. Deep wounds marred his body, and blood streamed from a gash along his temple, yet he did not fall.

Not yet.

Before him, a shadow loomed. A figure cloaked in shifting darkness, its face hidden behind a silver mask, its voice a whisper of nightmares. The shadow raised a jagged, cursed blade, its surface writhing as though it were alive.

"You were warned," the figure intoned, a voice like rusted steel. "And yet, you fought against fate."

Rhyven staggered, but his golden eyes burned with defiance. "I do not fear fate."

"You should."

The shadow struck.

The sword pierced through the king's chest, driving deep, its blackened edge pulsing with cursed energy. Rhyven's body stiffened, his lips parting in a silent gasp. Blood, dark and thick, spilled from his mouth. His knees buckled.

And then—the world shattered.

—-

Elyra's scream tore through the chamber as she was ripped back to the present. Her body convulsed, her limbs twitching uncontrollably as she collapsed onto the cold stone floor. Pain lanced through her skull, the aftershock of the vision searing into her mind like a brand.

Her breath came in ragged gasps. Her chest burned.

The vision had been clearer than any before. It had been vivid, raw, more real than anything she had ever seen.

And it could mean only one thing.

King Rhyven was doomed.

A sharp knock at the chamber door made Elyra jolt. She barely had the strength to push herself up onto her elbows when the heavy doors groaned open. A figure strode inside, dressed in the deep crimson robes of the Royal Sentinels. His face was shadowed beneath his hood, but there was no mistaking the authority in his stance.

"Oracle," the man spoke, his voice clipped. "The king summons you at once."

Elyra's heart lurched.

The king.

She had just seen his death. She had watched the life drain from his eyes, had felt the weight of his final breath.

And now, he was summoning her.

The omens had been right. Fate had already begun to move.

She rose unsteadily, pressing a hand against her forehead as if she could wipe away the remnants of the vision. "Did he say why?"

The sentinel hesitated before answering, "No, but he does not request. He commands."

Of course. Rhyven was a king. He was not a man accustomed to waiting.

Elyra steadied herself, adjusting the folds of her robe. Every part of her screamed to turn back, to ignore the summons, to pretend she had not seen what she had seen.

But fate had already taken hold.

And there was no escaping fate.

With a final deep breath, she stepped forward.

Two

Summoned to the Throne

The night air clung to Elyra like a second skin as she followed the Royal Sentinel through the labyrinthine corridors of the palace. The flickering torchlight cast long, wavering shadows along the stone walls, making the carved figures of warriors and kings seem alive, watching her with hollow eyes. Her footsteps were silent against the cold marble, but the pounding of her heart roared in her ears.

King Rhyven had summoned her.

Only moments ago, she had seen his death in a vision so vivid that the taste of iron still lingered on her tongue. She had watched the sword sink into his chest, had felt the unbearable weight of inevitability as the world shattered around him. And now, here she was, walking toward the man fate had marked for ruin.

The Sentinel before her did not speak, but she could feel the weight of his glances. She had been inside the palace before—many times, in fact—but never under such circumstances. The Oracle's role was to interpret the will of the gods, to guide the kingdom with wisdom and prophecy, not to stand before the king on a night like this, her soul heavy with a vision she did not wish to speak aloud.

They reached the grand double doors of the throne room. Towering slabs of wood, reinforced with iron, loomed before her. The Sentinel rapped his knuckles against the metal, the sound echoing through the corridor.

"Enter," a voice commanded from within.

Elyra swallowed hard as the doors groaned open.

The throne room was bathed in the dim glow of firelight, the massive iron chandelier casting dancing shadows against the towering stone pillars. At the center of the room, sitting upon his darkened throne, was King Rhyven.

He looked exactly as he had in her vision—his sharp golden eyes assessing her with unreadable intensity, his strong features carved from shadow and firelight. His black tunic was unadorned, a contrast to the heavy crimson cloak draped over his shoulders. A silver crown sat upon his dark hair, the intricate engravings glinting under the torchlight.

Elyra dropped to one knee, her hands pressed against the cool marble floor. "My king."

A beat of silence stretched between them before his voice rumbled through the room like distant thunder. "Rise, Oracle."

She obeyed, lifting her gaze to meet his. His stare was piercing, searching, as if he could see straight through her into the secrets she wished to keep buried.

"I assume you know why I have summoned you," he said, his tone measured.

Elyra hesitated.

She could tell him. She could spill the truth right now—that she had seen his death, that his fate was written in the blood of warriors and sealed by an unseen enemy. But something inside her urged caution.

To speak a prophecy before the right moment could be just as dangerous as withholding it.

"I do not," she answered carefully.

Rhyven's gaze flickered with something unreadable. "You are an Oracle, are you not?"

"Yes, my king."

"Then you should have seen that I had need of you."

Elyra's fingers curled into her robes, hidden from view. "The will of the gods is not always clear, Your Majesty. I see glimpses, not absolute truths."

The king studied her for a long moment before exhaling, leaning back against his throne. "Very well. You will tell me what you do see."

She forced herself to hold his gaze. "What is it you wish to know?"

Rhyven's jaw tensed, a flicker of something dark passing across his face before he spoke. "There are whispers of war. My enemies are gathering. I need to know what fate has in store for Kharoth."

Elyra's breath hitched.

War.

It had already begun.

The battlefield in her vision had not been of the past—it was the future. A war that would leave bodies strewn in its wake, and at its center, the king himself. His fall. His end.

She needed to be careful. She needed time to understand what she had seen, to unravel the meaning behind it.

"I will seek the gods' guidance, Your Majesty," she said, bowing her head. "But I must warn you—fate is not so easily swayed."

His expression darkened, something cold settling in his gaze.

"Fate is a coward's excuse."

Elyra flinched at his words, though she tried not to show it.

Rhyven rose from his throne, stepping down onto the marble floor. He was taller than she expected, his presence overwhelming. When he stopped before her, mere inches away, she felt the heat of his body, the quiet storm that surrounded him.

"I do not seek riddles or prayers," he said, his voice low but powerful. "I need certainty. I need to know if Kharoth will stand, or if I am to watch my kingdom crumble."

Elyra's breath came shallow.

She had to say something.

"You are right to be concerned, my king," she said carefully. "Darkness gathers. Enemies you do not yet see are moving in the shadows. The threads of fate are shifting—"

"Then tell me where they lead," he interrupted.

Elyra hesitated.

Straight to your death.

She could not say it. Not yet.

"Give me until dawn," she pleaded instead. "Allow me to seek further insight. I will perform the rites, speak to the gods. And then, I will tell you what I see."

Rhyven held her gaze for what felt like an eternity. She could feel the weight of his scrutiny, the slow unraveling of his patience.

Finally, he exhaled sharply. "Very well. But at first light, you will tell me the truth, Oracle. I will not tolerate deception."

Elyra bowed deeply. "Yes, my king."

The room fell silent, the firelight crackling softly in the background.

"You may go," Rhyven said at last.

Elyra turned, her steps slow and measured as she walked toward the great doors. But just as she reached them, his voice cut through the space between them, halting her in her tracks.

"One more thing, Oracle."

She turned back, her breath catching.

"Tell me," he said, his golden eyes locked onto hers. "Do you fear me?"

Elyra hesitated. The memory of his bloodied body flashed behind her eyes. The way he had clung to life even as fate dragged him toward death.

She held his gaze, her heartbeat steady despite the storm inside her.

"No," she said. "But you should fear what is to come."

For the first time, something flickered in Rhyven's expression—something uncertain, something unreadable.

Then, with a simple nod, he dismissed her.

Elyra stepped through the doors, the heavy wood groaning as they closed behind her.

The weight of her vision pressed against her shoulders, suffocating. She had bought herself time, but not much.

By dawn, she would have to tell him the truth.

And she had no idea if he would survive it.

Three

A Curse in Blood and Shadow

Elyra's footsteps echoed down the palace corridors, each step measured, each breath drawn with calculated control. The weight of her vision still pressed upon her chest like a leaden shroud. Dawn would come soon, and with it, the truth she could no longer withhold.

The king's fate was set.

Unless she found a way to change it.

The moment she stepped into her private chambers, she reached for the iron bowl resting atop a wooden stand, tipping its contents into the ceremonial brazier in the center of the room. Dried sage and crushed nightbloom tumbled into the waiting fire, sending up a plume of silver smoke that curled toward the ceiling like spectral fingers.

She dropped to her knees before the flames, the scent of burning herbs sharp in her nostrils.

"Show me," she whispered. "Show me what lies beneath the shadows. Show me the curse that binds the king."

The fire flickered. The world seemed to still.

Then, a whisper. A voice as ancient as time itself.

You already know.

Elyra's body tensed, her spine rigid. The voice did not come from the flames. It came from within her, deep and insidious, wrapping around her mind like unseen chains.

"No," she murmured. "I need to see more. I need to understand."

You understand enough.

The fire roared suddenly, the flames stretching high, their glow twisting and reshaping into something unnatural. Elyra inhaled sharply as the image began to form within the inferno.

A battlefield, just as before. But this time, she saw what came before the king's fall.

Blood. So much blood. And in its center, a man draped in dark robes, his hands painted with crimson, his face obscured by a silver mask. He was chanting, his voice dripping with something that was neither language nor spell, but something darker. Something forbidden.

The blood at his feet churned unnaturally, as if alive. It twisted, reshaping into symbols Elyra recognized—ancient markings of ruin, written in a script that predated even the gods. A curse.

The vision shifted.

The king as a child, no older than ten summers, standing before a great stone altar deep within the palace temple. The priests surrounded him, their hands raised in silent worship, their faces veiled. And then, a single figure stepped forward.

Not a priest. Not a man of faith.

A sorcerer.

He placed his hands upon the boy's head, whispering in that same vile tongue, his breath curling with dark mist. The young prince gasped, his golden eyes wide, his body shaking as the power seeped into his bones.

A curse woven into his blood. A curse destined to bloom the moment he claimed the throne.

Elyra jerked back from the fire, her breath ragged, her body trembling.

It wasn't just war that would kill Rhyven.

It was the curse.

It had always been the curse.

The king had never stood a chance.

A sharp knock at her door made her flinch. She scrambled to her feet, schooling her expression into something unreadable before stepping forward.

The door creaked open, revealing a familiar figure.

General Sareth.

The man was as imposing as ever, his armor polished to a sheen even in the dim light. His salt-and-pepper hair was cropped short, his scarred face hardened by decades of war. But tonight, his normally unshakable presence was… uneasy.

"You've been summoned," he said, his voice gruff.

Elyra studied him. "The king?"

Sareth nodded. "He awaits you in the temple."

Elyra's heart stuttered. The temple. The very place where the curse had first taken root.

The gods were weaving something tonight, whether she was ready for it or not.

She took a steadying breath. "I will come."

Sareth stepped aside as she passed, falling into step beside her as they made their way through the palace halls.

"You look troubled," he noted after a moment.

Elyra hesitated before answering. "And if I am?"

The general gave her a sidelong glance. "Then it is worse than I thought."

The words made a chill slither down her spine. "You suspected something?"

Sareth exhaled through his nose. "I was there the day his father died. I saw what happened. I saw how the late king bled from wounds that were never dealt by mortal hands." He glanced at her. "If you have seen something, Oracle, now is the time to speak it."

Elyra's fingers tightened around the folds of her robe. "Not yet."

Sareth grunted but said nothing more.

By the time they reached the temple doors, Elyra's pulse was a hammer against her ribs.

The temple was ancient, older than the palace itself. Tall marble pillars loomed over them, carved with prayers long forgotten. The heavy iron doors stood ajar, the braziers within flickering with ghostly blue flames.

She stepped inside.

And there, standing before the great altar, was Rhyven.

He was draped in ceremonial black, his cloak pooling at his feet like liquid shadow. The golden circlet rested upon his brow, catching the ethereal light. His hands were clasped behind his back, his posture rigid, his gaze locked onto the altar before him.

"You came," he said, without turning.

Elyra hesitated before stepping closer. "You summoned me, my king."

He finally turned then, his golden eyes piercing in the dim glow. "Do you know why I brought you here?"

Elyra swallowed. "Because you seek the truth."

His gaze did not waver. "Yes."

She took a breath, gathering herself. This was it. The moment she had been dreading.

"The truth is not kind, my king," she said, her voice steady. "Nor is it forgiving."

Rhyven took a slow step toward her. "Tell me anyway."

Elyra clenched her hands. "You are cursed."

Silence.

The word lingered between them, heavy and unrelenting.

Rhyven's expression did not change, but something in the air shifted. "A curse," he echoed, his voice dangerously quiet.

"Yes," she continued. "It was placed upon you as a child. A binding woven in blood and shadow. It has been waiting, dormant, until the day you took the throne."

Rhyven's jaw tightened. "And what does this curse demand?"

Elyra's throat went dry. "Your death."

The words shattered the space between them like a blade through glass.

For the first time, something flickered in the king's expression. Not fear. Not disbelief.

But rage.

Rage at the gods. At fate. At whatever cruel force had decided his life was not his own.

"You saw this," he said, his voice sharp as steel.

Elyra nodded. "I saw you fall."

Rhyven inhaled deeply, turning away. His hands curled into

fists at his sides, his body coiled with silent fury.

After a long moment, he spoke. "Can it be undone?"

Elyra hesitated. "I don't know."

He turned back to her, stepping closer. "Then find out."

His golden eyes burned with something unyielding, something dangerous. "Because I do not intend to die."

Elyra met his gaze, her heart hammering.

Neither did she.

Not if she could stop it.

Four

The Skeptical King

The silence between them was thick, pulsing like a living thing. The temple's dim glow flickered against the marble pillars, casting long, wavering shadows along the stone floor. Elyra could feel the weight of the king's gaze on her, golden eyes burning with barely restrained fury.

"A curse," Rhyven said, his voice a low growl. "You speak of it as though it is undeniable fact."

"It is," Elyra replied, steady despite the storm brewing before her. "The threads of fate do not lie."

Rhyven let out a sharp breath, stepping away from her. His boots echoed against the stone as he paced in slow, measured strides. "And yet," he muttered, "I have lived three decades and have never felt the touch of such magic. Why should I believe you now?"

Elyra resisted the urge to close her eyes, to steady herself before speaking again. She had expected this—his disbelief, his skepticism. The king was a man of war, of strategy and steel, not of prophecies and unseen forces.

But his doubt did not change the truth.

"You have felt it," she countered, watching him closely. "You just did not recognize it for what it was."

He halted mid-step, turning toward her. "Explain."

Elyra moved to the altar, running her fingers lightly over the ancient carvings etched into the stone. The markings pulsed faintly under her touch, the same script she had seen in her vision—the language of curses.

"You have never fallen in battle," she said, voice even. "Never suffered a wound that did not heal faster than expected. No sickness has ever touched you, no blade has ever taken your life, even when it should have. The curse was dormant, my king. A promise, waiting for the right moment to be fulfilled."

Rhyven was silent, but she saw the flicker of something behind his eyes.

Recognition.

Doubt.

"You think I was spared all these years only to meet an inevitable death now?" he said finally.

Elyra nodded. "The magic bound to you is old, woven deep into your bloodline. It is not a simple spell that can be undone with mere words. The curse was designed to awaken once you ascended the throne."

Rhyven exhaled sharply, running a hand through his dark hair. "And yet I still stand."

"Not for long," Elyra whispered.

His gaze snapped to hers, golden and fierce.

She did not falter.

"I saw you die," she said. "Not in sickness. Not by the hands of an assassin. You fell in battle, your blood spilling into the earth, your name lost to history."

Rhyven's jaw clenched, his shoulders tense beneath the weight of her words. He hated this—being told he was powerless against something he could not fight.

The king thrived in war, in challenges where steel met steel, where a man's fate could be decided by his own strength. But this? This was different.

This was a battle he could not win with a sword.

"I do not believe in fate," Rhyven said at last, voice edged with iron. "And I do not believe my destiny is written in ink I cannot erase."

"You can deny it all you want," Elyra said softly. "But the curse does not care for your disbelief."

He stared at her, unreadable. Then, without another word, he turned on his heel and strode away from the altar, his movements tight with frustration.

"Then tell me, Oracle," he said over his shoulder, voice laced with challenge. "If my death is inevitable, why tell me at all? Why not let fate take its course?"

Elyra stiffened.

Because she had not expected to care.

Because she had not expected the vision to shake her so completely.

Because—despite what she had seen—something deep within her refused to accept it.

She stepped toward him, lowering her voice. "Because I do not believe fate is absolute. I believe in choices. And right now, you have one."

He turned back to her, the firelight casting sharp shadows across his face. "And what choice is that?"

"To let the curse consume you." She met his gaze without fear. "Or to fight it."

Rhyven's lips curled into something almost amused, but there was no humor in his eyes. "Fight something I cannot see? Something I cannot strike down?"

"Yes," she said simply. "Because if you do not, you will die."

The words lingered between them, heavy and unrelenting.

Rhyven was silent for a long moment before he exhaled sharply, shaking his head. "You speak in riddles, Oracle."

Elyra stepped closer. "I speak the truth."

The king studied her, searching her face for any trace of deception. She held his gaze, unwavering.

Finally, he scoffed. "And what would you have me do? Pray? Beg the gods for mercy?" His tone was edged with sarcasm.

"No," Elyra said, her voice steady. "Let me help you."

His brow furrowed slightly, and for the first time, something flickered in his expression.

Curiosity.

"What do you propose?"

Elyra swallowed. "The curse was created with blood magic. It must be unraveled the same way. But to do that, I need to understand its source. I need to know who placed it upon you, why, and how deep it runs."

"And how do you intend to find that out?"

Elyra hesitated. "Through the temple archives. Through rituals far older than this kingdom."

Rhyven narrowed his eyes. "And if it cannot be undone?"

Elyra forced herself to breathe. "Then we find another way."

A dangerous silence stretched between them.

Then, unexpectedly, Rhyven laughed—a sharp, humorless sound.

"You ask me to believe in the impossible," he muttered.

Elyra lifted her chin. "You have survived impossible odds before, my king."

His golden eyes flickered with something unreadable.

For a long moment, she thought he would dismiss her, cast her out as nothing more than a fool clinging to shadows.

But then—

"You have until the next moonrise," he said, his voice a quiet command. "Find me proof of this curse. Show me something more than words."

Elyra's breath hitched.

A chance.

She bowed deeply. "I will not fail you."

Rhyven's gaze lingered on her a moment longer before he turned away, striding toward the doors of the temple.

Elyra watched him go, a quiet dread settling deep in her bones.

She had bought herself time.

But if she did not find the answers she sought, if she failed to prove to the king the truth of his own fate…

Then the next time she saw him, he would already be walking toward his death.

Five

Echoes of a Forgotten Past

The torches flickered low in the temple corridors, casting shifting shadows against the carved stone walls. Elyra walked quickly, her heart pounding in rhythm with her footsteps. The king had given her until the next moonrise to find proof of his curse, to show him something beyond mere words. But finding the origins of the magic that bound his fate would not be easy.

The curse had been set in blood and shadow long before his birth. And now, she had to reach back into history—back to a past even the gods had long abandoned.

She pulled her cloak tighter around her shoulders as she stepped deeper into the temple, past the grand altar where prayers had been whispered for centuries, past the endless corridors lined with statues of forgotten deities. This was a place of old power, but it was also a place of secrets.

And tonight, she needed one of them.

The archives lay beyond the inner sanctum, hidden beneath the temple's foundation. Few had access to it—only the High Priests, the Oracles, and those who had already been claimed by the gods. Elyra did not need permission. She had walked these halls long before she was given the title of Oracle. The knowledge within belonged to her as much as it did to the ancient stone that held it.

She pressed her palm against the cold surface of the iron door, whispering a single word in the old tongue. The runes carved into the metal flared with silver light before the locks clicked open.

Elyra slipped inside.

The air was thick with dust and the scent of aged parchment. The chamber stretched into darkness, shelves upon shelves of scrolls and tomes reaching toward the ceiling. The walls were carved with the symbols of those who had come before her, their names lost to time, but their wisdom buried within these texts.

She moved swiftly, fingers skimming over the spines of books that had not been touched in decades. She needed records from the reign of King Varyon—Rhyven's father. If the curse had been woven into the bloodline, it would have been recorded here.

Her fingers stopped on a thick, leather-bound tome. The edges were worn, the bindings cracked with age. It bore no title, but the symbol burned into its cover sent a chill down her spine.

The mark of the forgotten sorcerers.

A sect of magic-wielders who had once walked the lands of Kharoth before they had been purged from history. The same mark she had seen in her vision.

Elyra pulled the book free and carried it to the lone stone table at the center of the chamber. She opened it carefully, her breath held as she turned the brittle pages.

The words were written in the old tongue, but she understood them well.

The entries spoke of a deal made in desperation, of a king who sought to protect his bloodline from a fate worse than death. But the words were fragmented, the details obscured by time.

She turned the page—and her breath caught.

There, scrawled in faded ink, was an account of a night nearly three decades past.

The night of Rhyven's birth.

—-

"The king's firstborn shall be bound in blood and darkness. The bargain has been sealed. The price has been set. Only in death shall the debt be repaid."

—-

Elyra's fingers trembled as she traced the words.

The curse had not been placed by an enemy.

It had been placed by Rhyven's own father.

A sharp sound broke through the silence.

Elyra jerked her head up, her pulse spiking. The door to the archives stood slightly ajar, though she had locked it behind her.

Someone was here.

She rose swiftly, closing the book and pressing it against her chest. The shadows between the shelves stirred, but she saw no movement. Only silence. Only the press of something unseen, lurking just beyond the reach of the torchlight.

"Who's there?" she demanded, her voice steady despite the tension coiling in her spine.

No answer.

But the feeling remained.

She moved quickly, tucking the tome beneath her cloak before slipping between the shelves. The corridors of the temple were vast, but she knew them well. She took a passage through the side hall, her footsteps light against the stone.

The moment she stepped into the main corridor, a figure emerged from the shadows.

Elyra barely had time to react before a hand clamped around her wrist.

She twisted sharply, bringing her free hand up, a flicker of power sparking at her fingertips—but the grip was iron-strong.

"Oracle," a low voice murmured.

Her breath caught as she recognized the face.

General Sareth.

His scarred features were half-shrouded in darkness, but his grip did not loosen. His gaze flicked down to the tome hidden beneath her cloak, his expression unreadable.

"You shouldn't be here," he said.

Elyra lifted her chin. "Neither should you."

Sareth's lips pressed into a thin line. "The king does not take kindly to secrets being kept from him."

Elyra narrowed her eyes. "If you planned to stop me, you would have done so already."

Silence.

Then, to her surprise, Sareth released her wrist.

"Be careful with what you seek," he said, his voice quiet. "Not all truths deserve to be known."

Elyra hesitated for only a moment before slipping past him, her pulse hammering as she hurried toward the temple exit.

She had what she needed.

And now, she had to tell the king that his father had sealed his fate before he was even born.

—-

The night was still when Elyra reached the palace. The halls were quiet, the guards stationed outside the throne room standing rigid as she approached. They did not stop her.

She stepped inside, gripping the tome tightly.

Rhyven stood at the far end of the room, his back to her, his hands braced against the great war table where maps of the kingdom were spread. He did not turn as she entered.

"You're late," he said, his voice devoid of emotion.

Elyra swallowed, stepping closer. "I found something."

That made him turn. His golden eyes flicked to the book in her arms, then back to her face. "Show me."

Elyra placed the tome on the table and opened it to the passage she had found. The moment Rhyven's eyes scanned the words, she saw his jaw tighten, his fingers clenching against the edge of the table.

A muscle ticked in his temple. "You're certain this is real?"

Elyra nodded. "Your father made a deal to protect your bloodline, but it came with a cost. The curse is not simply misfortune—it is a debt, one that can only be repaid with your death."

The king's expression darkened.

For a long moment, he said nothing. Then, slowly, he exhaled.

"So that's it?" he muttered. "I was damned before I took my first breath."

Elyra hesitated. "Not necessarily."

Rhyven's gaze snapped to hers. "Explain."

She took a steady breath. "If the curse is a debt, then debts can be paid."

Rhyven's brow furrowed. "You just said the price is my life."

"Yes," Elyra said. "But what if there is another way?"

The firelight flickered between them.

Rhyven studied her, something unreadable flickering behind his golden eyes. "And you believe you can find it?"

Elyra met his gaze. "I have to."

Another silence stretched between them.

Then, Rhyven's lips curled into something almost dangerous. "Then let's see if fate can be cheated."

Elyra nodded.

Because she would not let fate claim him.

Not without a fight.

Six

Whispers of Rebellion

The silence that followed Elyra's revelation hung in the air like a blade suspended by a fraying thread. Rhyven's golden eyes flickered with unreadable emotion as he scanned the ancient text before him. The flames in the throne room cast shifting shadows across his sharp features, his jaw tense with the weight of what he had just learned.

Elyra waited.

She had laid the truth before him—the curse woven into his blood, the debt that demanded his death. And now, they stood on the edge of something far greater than either of them could yet understand.

A storm was coming.

And, deep in her bones, Elyra knew that the whispers of fate were growing louder.

Rhyven finally exhaled, his fingers tightening against the edge of the war table. "You believe there is another way," he said, his voice steady, yet laced with something dangerous.

"I do," Elyra replied, watching him closely.

His gaze snapped to hers, sharp as a blade. "Then find it."

She nodded. There was no other choice.

But even as the weight of their new alliance settled between them, a new tension pulled at the edges of the night. Something unseen. Something wrong.

And they were running out of time.

—-

The whispers started at dawn.

By midday, they had spread like wildfire.

Elyra stood at the high windows of the tower, overlooking the city below. The streets of Kharoth were alive with movement, merchants calling out their wares, citizens moving in hurried clusters, their voices hushed with unease.

She had felt it the moment she stepped outside the temple

that morning—an undercurrent in the air, something shifting beneath the surface of the kingdom.

Trouble was brewing.

Footsteps approached from behind, and she turned to find General Sareth stepping into the chamber. His expression was grim, his scarred face lined with tension.

"You've heard," he said without preamble.

Elyra nodded. "The people are restless."

Sareth exhaled sharply, crossing his arms over his broad chest. "More than restless. There are whispers spreading through the city—rumors of rebellion."

Elyra's stomach tightened.

She had expected resistance against the king, but not so soon.

"How much do we know?" she asked.

Sareth's jaw tensed. "Enough to be concerned. The nobles are uneasy, the high lords whispering behind closed doors. The merchants are grumbling over increased tariffs, and the soldiers—" He hesitated.

Elyra narrowed her eyes. "What about the soldiers?"

Sareth's voice was quieter when he spoke again. "There are

those among them who question their loyalty. Rhyven has ruled with strength, but fear is a fragile thing. If they sense weakness, they may turn against him."

The weight of his words settled heavily in her chest.

The king was already fighting a battle against fate itself.

And now, his own kingdom was beginning to turn against him.

Elyra glanced toward the city again, her mind racing. "If there is unrest among the soldiers, it means there is someone fanning the flames. This is no ordinary discontent."

Sareth nodded. "It's being orchestrated. And I have reason to believe that it may be coming from within the palace."

Elyra stiffened. "A traitor."

Sareth's gaze was unreadable. "Perhaps more than one."

A chill ran through her.

If there were those within the palace working against the king, then they were already a step behind.

"We need to move quickly," she said. "If rebellion is truly stirring, then we must find the source before it spreads."

Sareth gave a short nod. "I will have my men conduct quiet inquiries. If someone is conspiring against the king, we will root them out."

Elyra hesitated. "And the king?"

Sareth's jaw tightened. "He will not like this."

No, he wouldn't.

Rhyven was a warrior king, a ruler forged in battle. He did not tolerate weakness, and he certainly did not tolerate betrayal. If he learned that rebellion was growing within his own walls, he would strike first and ask questions later.

Elyra exhaled. "Then we do not tell him. Not until we know more."

Sareth studied her for a moment before giving a slow nod. "Agreed. But if this goes further than we suspect—"

"Then we tell him," Elyra finished. "Before it is too late."

Sareth turned to leave, his movements swift and precise. But just as he reached the door, he paused.

"There's one more thing," he said, glancing back at her.

Elyra frowned. "What is it?"

Sareth hesitated. "A message arrived this morning. From the outer provinces."

Elyra's pulse quickened. "And?"

Sareth's expression darkened. "The Eastern Warlords have broken their treaty."

The words hit her like a blow.

The war she had seen in her vision.

It was already beginning.

—-

The tension in the throne room was suffocating.

Rhyven stood at the center of it all, his presence a storm barely contained. His golden eyes burned as he listened to Sareth's report, his fingers curling into tight fists at his sides.

"So," he said, voice dangerously quiet, "not only do I have traitors within my own walls, but I now have war at my borders?"

Elyra watched him carefully, standing near the war table. She had known this moment would come, but it did not make it any easier.

Rhyven turned to Sareth, his expression unreadable. "How many?"

Sareth's tone was grim. "The Eastern Warlords have begun

assembling their forces near the river pass. Scouts report at least five battalions."

Rhyven's jaw clenched. "And our forces?"

"We are prepared," Sareth replied. "But if the soldiers are wavering in loyalty—"

"They will fight," Rhyven interrupted, his voice edged with iron.

Elyra felt the energy in the room shift.

This was what he knew.

War.

Battle.

This was where he thrived.

But fate had already shown her how this path would end.

If Rhyven went to war now, without breaking the curse, he would not return.

She stepped forward. "My king, we must proceed with caution."

His gaze snapped to her, sharp and unyielding. "Caution will not stop them from marching on my kingdom, Oracle."

"No," she said, "but walking into their trap will not save you either."

Silence.

The firelight flickered between them, illuminating the unspoken battle waging in his mind.

Finally, Rhyven exhaled sharply, turning away. "What would you have me do?"

Elyra hesitated.

This was the moment she had been waiting for—the moment where she could push him toward a different path.

"The rebellion is tied to this war," she said. "Someone is orchestrating this from the shadows. If we act too soon, we will be playing into their hands."

Rhyven's jaw tightened. "And if I wait too long, my enemies will overrun me."

"Then we do not wait," Elyra said. "We strike first—but not as they expect."

Rhyven turned back to her, something unreadable flickering in his gaze.

"Explain," he commanded.

Elyra took a steady breath. "Let me find the traitor within these walls. Let Sareth secure the loyalty of your men. And then—when we have rooted out those who seek to destroy you—we will strike with certainty, not desperation."

Rhyven studied her for a long moment.

Then, slowly, he nodded.

"You have until the rebellion reaches my gates," he said.

Elyra met his gaze, her heart hammering.

"Then let's begin," she whispered.

Because the war had already started.

And the battle for the king's fate had only just begun.

Seven

A Bargain with Fate

Elyra sat in the dim glow of her chamber's single oil lamp, the ancient tome spread open before her. The thick leather cover, cracked with age, held the secrets she sought. Words in the forgotten tongue danced on the pages, their shapes jagged and unnatural. With each phrase she deciphered, the weight of the curse seemed to press more heavily upon her chest.

It had been hours since she'd last seen Rhyven. He had returned to the war council, leaving her with a single command: find something—anything—that might unravel the curse. It was a monumental task, made more difficult by the lingering echoes of her own visions. Each time she closed her eyes, she could see his blood staining the earth, the darkness coiling around him as he fell. The images haunted her, drove her to keep reading even as exhaustion clawed at her.

She brushed her fingers across a passage that caught her attention. The words seemed to shimmer under the flickering lamplight:

The bargain is sealed in blood. To unbind it, one must face the Shadow Between Worlds.

Elyra's breath hitched. The Shadow Between Worlds. A place whispered of in the oldest myths—a realm where the boundaries of life and death, reality and illusion, blurred. Few had ever ventured there. Fewer still had returned. It was said to be a domain of broken truths and endless torment, a price that only the desperate would pay. If the curse on Rhyven's bloodline was tied to this place, then breaking it would require more than knowledge or power. It would require a gamble against fate itself.

She pushed back from the table and rose to her feet, her thoughts racing. The mention of the Shadow felt like a revelation, but it also filled her with dread. She would need to tell Rhyven, to warn him of the price that might come with any attempt to unbind the curse. Yet she also knew that she would have to be careful. Rhyven was a man who trusted action over words, strength over caution. He would not be easily persuaded to tread a path fraught with unknown dangers.

The door to her chamber creaked open, breaking her train of thought. Sareth stepped inside, his armor clinking softly in the silence. He looked tired, more so than she had ever seen him. The lines on his face seemed deeper, his expression grim.

"They're moving faster than we expected," he said without preamble. "The rebellion is no longer a whisper. It's growing. We've received word that several garrisons in the outer territories have declared their allegiance to a shadow council."

Elyra's heart sank. "A shadow council?"

Sareth nodded. "We don't know who they are—yet. But their reach is spreading. If we don't act soon, the king will face an army not just from the east, but from within his own borders."

Elyra clenched her fists, her nails biting into her palms. The pieces were falling into place, but they painted a picture she had hoped to avoid. The curse, the rebellion, the shadow council—it was all connected. And now the kingdom was teetering on the brink of collapse.

"I found something," she said, her voice low. "Something that might explain how to break the curse."

Sareth's eyes narrowed. "Go on."

She hesitated. "The curse was bound through a bargain, sealed in blood. To undo it, someone must enter a place known as the Shadow Between Worlds."

Sareth's frown deepened. "The Shadow? I've heard the name in passing, from old soldiers who spoke of it in hushed tones. They called it a death trap, a realm where no man returns whole—if he returns at all."

Elyra nodded. "It's dangerous, yes. But it may be the only way to sever the bond that holds Rhyven's fate in its grip."

The general was silent for a long moment, his gaze heavy. "And you plan to tell the king this?"

"I must."

Sareth grunted, crossing his arms. "You know how he is. If you tell him there's a path to break the curse, he'll take it, no matter the cost."

Elyra lowered her head. "I know."

"Then you'd best be sure it's worth the risk," Sareth said before turning toward the door. "He'll want answers. Make sure you have them."

—-

When Elyra finally stood before Rhyven, the weight of her discovery pressed heavily on her shoulders. The king was seated at the war table, his golden eyes scanning a map of the kingdom. His expression was a mask of determination, but she could sense the tension beneath it.

"You have news," he said without looking up.

"I do." She stepped closer, her voice steady despite the rapid beat of her heart. "I've found a way to break the curse."

That caught his attention. His gaze snapped to hers, sharp and intense. "You're certain?"

"I've found a lead," she clarified. "But it's not without risk."

Rhyven stood, towering over the table. "What kind of risk?"

She met his gaze. "The curse was tied to a bargain made long ago. To unbind it, we must face the force that holds it together—the Shadow Between Worlds."

His eyes narrowed. "And what, exactly, is this Shadow?"

"It's a place that exists beyond our realm," Elyra explained. "A realm where the barriers between life and death, reality and illusion, dissolve. Those who enter rarely return, and those who do are often… changed."

Rhyven's jaw tightened. "And you believe this is the only way?"

"It's the only way I've found so far," she admitted. "If we want to sever the curse at its source, we must confront the Shadow."

Rhyven turned away, his hands braced on the edge of the table. "I've faced countless battles, survived odds that should have killed me. But this… this sounds like madness."

"It may be," Elyra said quietly. "But if we do nothing, the curse will claim you. You saw what happened to your father. This will not stop on its own."

He was silent for a long moment, his broad shoulders tense. Finally, he turned back to her, his golden eyes piercing. "If we do this, if we take this gamble, what's the cost?"

Elyra hesitated. "The Shadow will demand something in return. It always does. But until we enter, I can't say what that price will be."

The room fell into an uneasy silence. The flickering torches cast long shadows across the walls, as if the chamber itself held its breath.

Rhyven straightened, his expression hardening. "Then we prepare. You've brought me the path. I'll walk it. If this is the only way to break the curse, then so be it."

Elyra's breath caught. She had hoped for more time, for another option. But Rhyven had made his choice. He was a man who faced challenges head-on, who refused to bend before threats, even when they came from the unknown.

"Then I will guide you," she said softly. "But you must trust me. The Shadow is not like anything you've faced before. It can twist your thoughts, your memories. It will try to break you."

Rhyven's expression didn't waver. "It won't."

Elyra wished she shared his certainty. But as she looked into his eyes, she saw something that steadied her—resolve. He would not face this alone. She would stand beside him, no matter what awaited them.

The Shadow loomed ahead, a force of fate and chaos.

And they were going to bargain with it.

51

Eight

The Touch of the Forbidden

Elyra paced the confines of her chamber, the silence of the palace heavy around her. Somewhere, deep in the recesses of the great stone halls, she could hear the low hum of distant voices—guards exchanging clipped words, servants moving in whispered steps. But within her room, it was just her, the lamplight, and the relentless echoes of her own thoughts.

The air was colder tonight, a chill that seeped through the heavy stone walls and seemed to coil around her ankles. She had long since abandoned her seat by the small wooden desk, the half-read tome left open, its ancient script swimming before her tired eyes. The symbols etched into the pages felt more ominous with every glance, their meaning tangled in layers she wasn't sure she could ever fully unravel.

Her mind refused to settle. The Shadow Between Worlds. The bargain it demanded. The unknown price. It was all tied together—Rhyven's curse, the growing rebellion, the murmurs of betrayal within the palace. And yet, as she tried to piece it all together, one thought pulled at her more insistently than the rest: the king himself.

She could still see him as he had stood in the war room, his golden eyes alight with determination. He had spoken with such certainty, with the kind of resolve that should have been reassuring. Instead, it unsettled her. She had warned him of the dangers. She had told him what the Shadow could do, how it could twist the mind, warp reality, destroy a person from within. And still, he had said he would face it.

Elyra stopped her pacing and rested a hand against the cool stone wall. The rough texture grounded her for a moment, but her thoughts continued to race. Why did it bother her so much? She had done her duty—delivered the truth, offered her guidance. Whatever happened next was up to him.

Yet, the image of Rhyven standing alone before the Shadow wouldn't leave her.

She didn't hear the door open.

"Restless?"

The voice startled her, low and familiar. She turned sharply to find Rhyven standing in the doorway, his tall frame half-lit by the flickering light of the corridor torches. His expression was unreadable, but his presence filled the room in an instant.

"I could ask the same of you," Elyra replied, her voice steadier than she felt.

He stepped inside without invitation, closing the door behind him. "I thought you might have more to tell me. Something you didn't say earlier."

Elyra's fingers tightened against the wall. "I told you all I know. I don't withhold information, especially not on matters as important as this."

Rhyven's gaze lingered on her, golden and piercing. "No one tells everything, Oracle. Not all at once."

She met his stare, refusing to flinch. "I've told you what I've seen. What I've read. If I'd found another way, I would have told you that as well."

A faint smile flickered at the corners of his mouth, though it didn't reach his eyes. "You seem tense."

"Perhaps that's because I'm trying to keep you alive," she shot back before she could stop herself.

For a moment, the air between them was thick with unspoken tension. Then, to her surprise, Rhyven chuckled. It was a low, quiet sound, devoid of true humor.

"You have a fire in you," he said, taking a step closer.

Elyra moved away from the wall, her pulse quickening. "You didn't come here to talk about me."

"No," he admitted, his tone softening. "I came because I wanted to understand something. You've seen my death, haven't you?"

Her heart clenched. "Yes."

"And you believe it's inevitable?"

"I believe that if the curse isn't broken, it will happen."

He tilted his head, studying her. "But you also believe there's a way out. That we can cheat fate."

She hesitated. "I believe that choices can change the course of destiny. But the cost—"

"Will be worth it," he said firmly.

Elyra frowned. "You can't know that."

"And you can't know that it won't."

She exhaled sharply, frustration curling in her chest. "This isn't a battlefield, Rhyven. You can't win this with sheer force of will."

"Then what can I win it with?" he asked, stepping closer still. His voice dropped, quieter now, yet carrying an intensity that made her blood run faster. "What do you suggest I do, Oracle?

Sit back and let the curse claim me? Let this rebellion tear my kingdom apart? Tell me—what would you have me do?"

Elyra's breath caught. He was too close now, the heat of his presence tangible. The golden light from the lamp softened his sharp features, but it did nothing to dim the fire in his eyes.

"You should trust that I'm trying to help you," she said, her voice quieter.

"And you should trust that I'll do whatever it takes to save my kingdom," he replied.

For a moment, neither of them spoke. The silence was thick, charged. Elyra could feel her heart racing, her pulse quickening as his gaze held hers. There was something dangerous about him, something that made her want to look away but kept her rooted in place.

"You speak as if you already know the outcome," he said at last. "As if you've already seen it all."

"I've seen enough," she whispered.

Rhyven's lips curved into a faint, almost predatory smile. "Then you know that I don't give in easily."

She did know that. She had seen his stubbornness, his resolve, his refusal to bow to anything—not to enemies, not to curses, not even to fate itself.

And it terrified her.

"Rhyven—"

Her voice faltered as he reached out, his hand brushing against hers. It was the barest contact, just the tips of his fingers against her knuckles, but it sent a jolt through her like lightning.

"You think this is all about a curse," he murmured, his voice low. "But it's not, is it?"

Elyra's breath hitched. "I don't know what you mean."

He leaned in slightly, his golden eyes searching hers. "I think you do."

For a moment, she couldn't move, couldn't breathe. Her mind raced, trying to grasp what was happening, trying to understand the undercurrent that had suddenly shifted between them.

But then he stepped back, breaking the spell. The heat that had coiled in her chest faded, replaced by the cold reality of the room.

"I'll trust you, Oracle," he said, his tone even. "For now."

He turned and walked toward the door, his presence leaving a hollow space in the room.

Elyra stared after him, her thoughts a tangled mess. The touch of his hand still lingered on her skin, the weight of his gaze still burned in her mind.

When the door closed behind him, she let out a shaky breath and pressed her fingers against her temples.

Rhyven was dangerous, not just because of the curse, not just because of the rebellion.

He was dangerous because he made her feel something she couldn't afford to feel.

And that, more than anything, frightened her.

Nine

The Oracle's Betrayal

The cold morning air whispered through the towering halls of the palace, slipping through stone arches and over marble floors. Elyra could feel it even here, deep within the sanctity of the Oracle's chamber. She stood at her writing desk, staring down at a blank parchment. The ink in her quill was dark and ready, yet her hand trembled ever so slightly above the page.

She had not slept since Rhyven's last visit. The memory of his touch, brief as it had been, lingered in her mind. But it was not only his presence that kept her awake. It was the decision that loomed over her—the one she had made before the sun rose.

There were whispers in the palace. She had heard them in passing from servants, seen the unease in Sareth's eyes, felt the tension in Rhyven's shoulders. The rebellion was more than a distant rumor now. It was here, inside these walls. The shadow council's influence was spreading, turning soldiers against their king, planting seeds of doubt among the noble houses. And Elyra, the Oracle trusted to guide the kingdom, now found herself at a crossroads.

Her decision had been made hours ago. The Shadow Between Worlds, the price it demanded, the dangers that lay within—she knew Rhyven was walking toward his death. The curse was tied to more than just his bloodline. It was tied to the kingdom itself, a thread that ran through the heart of Kharoth. If the king fell, the rebellion would not end. The shadow council would rise, and the kingdom would fracture beyond repair.

She dipped her quill into the ink and began to write.

—-

The sun had barely risen when the first whispers of betrayal reached Rhyven's ears.

He stood in the war room, his eyes scanning a map spread out before him. Sareth had just returned from the outer territories, bringing news that several garrisons had sworn allegiance to the shadow council. The king's jaw was set, his golden eyes burning with controlled fury.

"This rebellion is no longer in the shadows," Rhyven said, his voice low. "They've taken two of our strongest border fortresses without a fight. What does that tell you?"

Sareth's face was grim. "It tells me someone within the palace is feeding them information."

Rhyven straightened, his fists curling against the edge of the table. "A traitor."

"More than one, I'd wager," Sareth said. "The speed at which they've moved—these plans have been in place for months. Years, perhaps. Someone close to the throne is working against you."

Rhyven's gaze darkened. "Find them."

Sareth hesitated. "My king, if I may…"

"Speak."

Sareth's voice lowered. "I've heard rumors—whispers about the Oracle. They say she's been seen meeting with figures who have no place in the palace. Some claim she's been in contact with those outside our borders."

Rhyven's expression was stone. "You mean to suggest that Elyra—"

"I mean to say that you should consider every possibility, Your Majesty," Sareth interrupted. "Even those that seem unthinkable."

Rhyven turned sharply to face him. "Elyra has guided this kingdom for years. She's been loyal—"

"Loyal to what?" Sareth asked quietly. "The gods? The throne? Or something else entirely?"

For a long moment, neither man spoke. The tension in the room was palpable, the air heavy with unspoken doubts.

Rhyven exhaled sharply, turning back to the map. "I'll hear no more of it until we have proof. Find the traitor. But leave Elyra out of this."

Sareth inclined his head, though his expression remained troubled. "As you wish, Your Majesty."

—-

Elyra's parchment was finished. The words she had written seemed to glow in the dim light of her chamber, as if the ink itself carried a weight she could not lift. She stared at the message for what felt like an eternity before finally rolling it into a scroll and sealing it with wax.

She knew what would happen once this reached its intended recipient. Kharoth would not survive the rebellion if it continued unchecked. Rhyven's fate had been sealed the moment he took the throne. If the shadow council succeeded in toppling him, the kingdom would fall into chaos, and the curse would devour whatever remained.

But this was her choice now. She had made a bargain—not with the Shadow Between Worlds, but with the shadow council itself. The council's emissary had come to her days ago, slipping into her chambers under the cover of darkness. They had promised that if she helped them, they would spare the kingdom from complete destruction. The rebellion would end quickly, the bloodshed minimal. The kingdom would survive. But Rhyven would not.

Her betrayal was not driven by hatred or ambition. It was driven by necessity. The kingdom was larger than its king. A single life, even that of a ruler, was a small price to pay to ensure the survival of thousands.

Elyra opened her chamber door and stepped into the corridor. The palace was still quiet, though the guards patrolled more frequently now. She moved quickly, her heart pounding as she approached the drop point. In a secluded alcove near the eastern tower, a small box had been placed—the means by which she would deliver her message. She slid the scroll inside, her fingers trembling as she closed the lid.

She lingered for a moment, her breathing shallow. There was still time to retrieve it, to undo what she had set into motion. But the faces of the people came to her mind—the merchants in the streets, the children playing in the courtyards, the farmers who relied on the kingdom's stability to survive. She could not let them be swallowed by the curse's darkness.

She turned away from the box and began to walk back to her chambers. Each step felt heavier than the last, as though the walls themselves knew what she had done. She reached her door and slipped inside, shutting out the rest of the palace.

It was done.

Elyra sank into her chair, her hands shaking. She had betrayed the king. She had betrayed his trust, his resolve, the fragile hope he had placed in her guidance.

But she had done it for the kingdom. For the people.

Hadn't she?

—-

That night, the palace was alive with whispers. The shadow council's plans were advancing, and the rebellion moved closer to the heart of Kharoth. Rhyven remained in the war room, his mind consumed with strategies and countermeasures. He trusted no one fully, not even his closest advisors. And yet, when he thought of Elyra, a part of him resisted the doubt that Sareth had planted. She had always been there, the Oracle who spoke the truth even when it was difficult to hear.

He had no way of knowing that in her chambers, Elyra sat alone, her hands still trembling, as she waited for the inevitable repercussions of her choice. The betrayal was done, the message delivered.

All she could do now was pray that the price she had paid would be enough to save them all.

Ten

A Kiss That Changes Destiny

The night was unnaturally quiet, the stillness that could only be born of tension too heavy for the world to bear. A single torch burned low in the corridor outside Elyra's chambers, its feeble light flickering against the cold stone walls. Inside, she stood by the narrow window, staring into the darkness. The shadow council's forces moved somewhere beyond the horizon, gathering strength. Within these walls, the tension between loyalty and betrayal simmered just below the surface.

She hadn't slept in days. Each time she closed her eyes, she felt the weight of the scroll she'd sent, the message that had put into motion events she could no longer control. The shadow council would act soon. Rhyven would face them. And the curse—always the curse—hung over everything like a storm waiting to break.

She turned from the window, the hem of her robes whispering against the stone floor. Her chest felt heavy, her thoughts a labyrinth of doubt and fear. She had made her choice. She had acted in what she believed was the kingdom's best interest. And yet, the image of Rhyven's eyes—those sharp, golden eyes— kept returning to her. He trusted her. Despite the tensions that strained their relationship, he had believed in her visions, her guidance.

And she had betrayed him.

A soft knock startled her. Elyra froze, her heart leaping into her throat. Before she could call out, the door opened. Rhyven stepped inside, closing the heavy door behind him. The flickering torchlight from the corridor painted his face in shadows, but his gaze found hers immediately, piercing and unyielding.

"My king," she began, but her voice wavered.

Rhyven held up a hand, silencing her. "You've avoided me for days, Elyra."

"I've been—"

"Busy," he finished, his tone sharp. "You've said that before. But what I need now is clarity. Truth."

She swallowed hard, her fingers curling into the fabric of her robes. "What truth do you seek?"

He moved closer, his presence filling the room. Rhyven had a way of commanding attention without effort, his every step measured, his every movement deliberate. He stopped just a few paces from her, close enough that she could feel the heat of his body in the cold chamber.

"I need to know," he said, his voice low, "if you still believe I can win."

Elyra's heart pounded painfully against her ribs. The weight of her betrayal pressed down on her like an iron chain. She had to choose her words carefully. "I believe you are a strong king," she said carefully. "But this fight—this rebellion, this curse—"

"Stop," Rhyven interrupted. His gaze bore into hers, sharp and demanding. "No riddles. No vague prophecies. Just tell me. Do you believe in me?"

The room felt impossibly small. Elyra's hands trembled at her sides, her throat dry. She had seen his death. She had sent the message that would bring his enemies to his doorstep. She had tried to save the kingdom, but now, face-to-face with the man she had betrayed, she felt the enormity of her decision crushing down on her.

"Yes," she whispered at last, her voice barely audible.

Rhyven stepped closer, and she found herself unable to move. His golden eyes searched hers, and for a moment, the weight of his authority seemed to lift. He wasn't a king at that moment— not entirely. There was something else in his gaze, something that made her breath catch.

"You don't have to carry this alone," he said, his voice softer now. "I see it in your eyes, Elyra. The fear. The doubt. Tell me what burdens you."

She shook her head, her throat tightening. "I can't."

"You can," Rhyven insisted. His hand rose, hesitating for a fraction of a second before it rested lightly on her shoulder. The warmth of his touch sent a jolt through her, and she felt her carefully constructed defenses begin to crack. "Whatever it is, you don't have to face it alone."

Elyra's chest heaved, the weight of her guilt and fear pressing down on her. The truth was a dagger poised to strike, and she knew that once it was revealed, nothing would be the same. But she couldn't say it. She couldn't admit what she had done—not here, not now.

Her silence spoke volumes.

Rhyven's hand moved to her chin, tilting her face up so that she was forced to meet his gaze. His touch was firm, but not harsh. His expression had softened, the sharp lines of his jaw relaxed. In his eyes, she saw a flicker of something she couldn't name—something that made her heart ache.

"You've fought for this kingdom," he said quietly. "You've guided me, warned me, given me the strength to keep going. You may think you're just the Oracle, but you're more than that. To me, you're…" His voice trailed off, the words lingering unspoken in the air.

Time seemed to slow. The space between them was a fragile thing, a delicate thread that connected them in a way Elyra hadn't realized until now. Rhyven's fingers brushed against her cheek, and she felt her breath hitch. The world beyond the chamber faded, the rebellion, the curse, the shadow council—all of it dissolved into the background.

The only thing that mattered was this moment.

And then, he kissed her.

It was not a hesitant kiss, nor was it rough. It was deliberate, a firm yet gentle act that left no room for uncertainty. His lips were warm against hers, his hand steady as it cupped her face. Elyra's mind reeled, her body frozen for a heartbeat before she found herself leaning into him, her hands clutching at his tunic. The kiss deepened, and for a brief, fleeting moment, the weight of the world lifted.

She felt something shift within her—a spark, a surge of heat that coursed through her veins. The visions she had seen, the fate she had tried to change, seemed to fade into the background. In that instant, there was no rebellion, no curse. Only him.

But the moment was fleeting.

As they parted, Elyra's chest tightened. The guilt returned with a vengeance, sharper now than before. She stared at him, her heart pounding, her mind screaming at her to say something, to confess.

Rhyven's gaze held hers, and a faint smile touched his lips. "You don't have to be afraid, Elyra. We'll face whatever comes together."

Her stomach churned. He trusted her. He believed in her.

And she had betrayed him.

Elyra turned away, her hands trembling as she pressed them against the cool stone of the window ledge. "You don't understand," she whispered.

"Then help me understand," Rhyven said gently. "Whatever it is, I can handle it."

Tears pricked at her eyes, but she refused to let them fall. "Some things… some things can't be undone."

The silence stretched, heavy and unrelenting. Elyra felt Rhyven's presence behind her, strong and steady. He didn't press her further, didn't demand answers. Instead, he simply stood there, waiting.

And she knew that when the truth finally came to light, when he learned what she had done, it would shatter whatever fragile connection they had just forged.

But for now, in the quiet aftermath of the kiss that should never have happened, she allowed herself a single moment of selfish hope—that maybe, just maybe, they could still find a way to change destiny.

Eleven

The Assassin's Blade

Night had settled over the palace, casting long shadows across the marble corridors. The distant murmur of the wind echoed through the stone halls, a low, mournful sound that seemed to warn of dangers unseen. The torches that lined the walls flickered weakly, their light barely reaching into the corners where darkness pooled, deep and forbidding.

Elyra moved quickly and quietly, her robes whispering against the floor as she made her way toward the king's chambers. The events of the day still weighed heavily on her—Rhyven's unwavering confidence, the rebellion's growing strength, and the memory of the kiss that still lingered on her lips. She had tried to push the thought aside, tried to focus on the curse and the rebellion, but the moment haunted her, pulling at her like a thread threatening to unravel everything she thought she understood.

She shook her head, trying to banish the memory. Now was not the time for distraction. The information she carried was too important. Sareth had discovered a lead on the traitor within the palace, a name whispered among the soldiers: Seron. A shadowy figure with ties to the rebellion, one who had been seen near the council chambers at odd hours, slipping in and out like a ghost. Elyra needed to warn Rhyven immediately. If Seron was truly the one feeding information to the shadow council, then he had to be stopped before more harm could be done.

The corridor leading to the king's chambers was eerily silent. The guards who normally stood watch were absent, their posts abandoned. Elyra's heart quickened as unease crept over her. She slowed her steps, her senses alert. Something was wrong. The stillness wasn't natural.

She reached the large double doors that marked the entrance to Rhyven's chambers. One door was ajar, just enough to let a sliver of dim light escape into the corridor. Elyra hesitated, her hand hovering near the handle. She could feel the hairs on the back of her neck rise, a primal instinct warning her that danger was near.

Pushing the door open slowly, Elyra stepped inside. The room was dimly lit, the embers in the fireplace glowing faintly. The heavy velvet curtains were drawn shut, trapping the warmth of the fire inside. Rhyven's bed lay empty, the covers undisturbed. The room seemed untouched, yet the air was thick with tension, as though the walls themselves were holding their breath.

"Your Majesty?" Elyra called softly, her voice barely more than a whisper.

No answer.

She stepped further inside, her eyes scanning every corner. The sitting area by the fire was vacant, the heavy chair pushed back as if someone had left in a hurry. A goblet sat on the nearby table, still half full, the wine within glinting in the firelight. Something glinted next to it—a dagger, its blade slim and wickedly sharp, resting on the edge of the table. But it wasn't one of Rhyven's ceremonial blades. This dagger was foreign, the hilt adorned with unfamiliar symbols.

Elyra's breath hitched. She knew without a doubt: this was no ordinary weapon.

She reached for the dagger, her fingers brushing the cold metal. A chill ran down her spine as she lifted it, the weight of the blade heavier than it should have been. This was not a tool of war—it was a tool of murder, crafted for precision, for silence.

And it had been left here, as if someone wanted it to be found.

A sudden noise shattered the stillness—a faint creak of a floorboard from the adjoining chamber. Elyra spun, the dagger still in her hand. Her heart thundered in her chest as she crept toward the source of the sound. The door to the adjoining room was ajar, the sliver of darkness beyond it beckoning her forward.

She pushed the door open slowly, revealing the king's private study. The room was darker than the bedchamber, the only light coming from a single candelabra on the desk. Papers and maps were strewn across the surface, evidence of Rhyven's tireless efforts to stay one step ahead of the rebellion. But he was not here. The room appeared empty.

Yet Elyra felt it again—that prickle at the back of her neck, the undeniable sensation of being watched.

A shadow moved near the far wall, almost imperceptible, but Elyra's sharp eyes caught it. She gripped the dagger tightly, her pulse quickening. The shadow shifted, and a figure emerged from the darkness. The man was cloaked, his face obscured by a hood. He moved silently, his steps deliberate and fluid, like a predator stalking its prey.

Elyra's voice caught in her throat. "Who are you?" she demanded, though her voice wavered.

The figure did not answer. Instead, he stepped closer, the dim candlelight catching the glint of a blade in his hand—longer than hers, curved and wicked. The air grew colder, and Elyra felt her grip on the dagger tighten.

"Why are you here?" she pressed, trying to keep her voice steady. "What do you want?"

Still no answer. The assassin advanced, his movements calculated, his silence more threatening than any words could be.

Elyra's mind raced. This wasn't just a random intruder. This was someone who had come with purpose—someone who had come for Rhyven. But the king was nowhere to be found, and now the assassin's attention was fixed on her.

She took a step back, then another, her eyes never leaving the hooded figure. She could feel the stone wall behind her now, the solid barrier offering no escape. Her breath came in shallow gasps as the assassin closed the distance. He moved like a shadow, his blade poised, his intent clear.

In that moment, Elyra knew she was no warrior. She had no training, no experience with weapons. She was an Oracle, not a soldier. The dagger in her hand felt foreign, its weight unfamiliar. But she also knew that if she hesitated, if she faltered for even a second, she would not survive.

As the assassin lunged, Elyra acted on instinct. She raised the dagger, deflecting his strike just enough to avoid a fatal blow. The clash of blades rang out, sharp and jarring in the otherwise silent room. Pain lanced through her arm as his blade nicked her, but she didn't stop. She twisted, slipping past him, putting distance between them.

"Help!" she shouted, her voice echoing off the stone walls. "Guards!"

The assassin didn't pause. He lunged again, and Elyra barely managed to dodge. Her heart pounded as she fought to keep him at bay, each movement clumsy yet desperate. She could see his face now—partially visible beneath the hood. Cold, emotionless, focused entirely on his task.

Her foot caught on the edge of the rug, and she stumbled. The assassin seized the moment, closing in with his blade raised. Elyra's breath caught as she braced for the final strike.

But then, from behind the assassin, a flash of steel. A familiar voice, sharp and commanding.

"Step away from her!"

Rhyven.

The king moved with the precision of a seasoned warrior, his sword cutting through the air as he struck at the assassin. The hooded man barely had time to react, his blade meeting Rhyven's with a resounding clash. Elyra scrambled back, her hands trembling as she watched the fight unfold.

Rhyven's strikes were relentless, his movements fluid and deliberate. The assassin fought fiercely, but the king's skill and sheer will overwhelmed him. With a final, powerful blow, Rhyven disarmed the intruder. The assassin fell to his knees, his weapon clattering to the floor.

Guards burst into the room, their armor gleaming in the dim light. They quickly subdued the hooded man, dragging him away as he struggled against their grip. The room fell silent once more, save for the sound of Elyra's labored breathing.

Rhyven turned to her, his golden eyes searching her face. "Are you hurt?"

Elyra nodded faintly, clutching her arm where the blade had grazed her. "I'm fine," she managed, though her voice was shaky. "But you… you weren't here…"

Rhyven's expression darkened. "I suspected something was amiss when the guards left their posts. I stepped away to investigate. I didn't expect to return to this."

Elyra swallowed hard, the realization sinking in. The assassin had come for him. She had been caught in the crossfire, a moment of chance that had brought her face to face with death.

As Rhyven helped her to her feet, his grip firm and steady, Elyra's mind raced. The rebellion, the curse, the traitor within the palace walls—it was all converging. And now, more than ever, she knew that their fight was just beginning.

Twelve

The Rift Between Us

Rhyven was silent as the guards dragged the hooded assassin from his chambers, his golden eyes fixed on the stone floor. The quiet that followed was oppressive, every second stretching into an eternity. Elyra stood a few steps away, her arm still stinging from the shallow cut she'd sustained during the struggle. The weight of everything—her visions, her choices, the rebellion brewing outside these walls—pressed down on her, threatening to crush her completely.

When the doors closed behind the guards, Rhyven turned to her. His gaze wasn't sharp this time; it was distant, as though his thoughts had traveled somewhere she couldn't follow. The usual fire in his eyes had dimmed, replaced by something heavier, something darker.

"You could have been killed," he said at last, his voice low.

Elyra flinched. The words weren't loud, but they carried an edge that cut deeper than a shout. She had no immediate response, no reassurance to offer. Because the truth was, she could have died. The assassin's blade had been mere inches from her heart before Rhyven intervened.

"I—" she started, but the words died on her lips.

"You shouldn't have been here," Rhyven continued, his tone sharper now. "If I hadn't returned when I did—"

"I'm sorry," Elyra interrupted, her voice firmer than she expected. "I didn't know you weren't here. I came because I thought you needed to know something."

He crossed his arms, his gaze never leaving hers. "And what was so important that you came to my chambers in the middle of the night?"

Elyra hesitated. The information about Seron and his possible connection to the rebellion felt like a distant concern compared to what had just happened. But she had come to warn him, and she had to see it through.

"There's a name," she said finally. "One whispered among the guards. Seron. He may be connected to the rebellion, perhaps even the shadow council. I thought you needed to know before—before anything else happened."

Rhyven's expression didn't change. He stood there, unmovable as stone, the weight of his scrutiny pressing down on her. The silence stretched until it became unbearable.

"Seron," he said at last. "And you believe this name is tied to the council?"

"Yes," Elyra said quickly. "At least, that's what I've heard. I thought—"

"You thought you could handle this on your own," he cut in, his voice low but cutting. "You thought you'd bring this information to me without any thought of your own safety. And now look what's happened."

Elyra's temper flared despite the circumstances. "I wasn't handling it on my own. I was trying to help you."

"By putting yourself in danger?" he shot back. "By walking into my chambers alone in the middle of the night, without knowing what or who might be waiting for you?"

She stepped closer, her own voice rising. "I didn't know the guards had left their posts. I didn't know you wouldn't be here. I came because I thought it was urgent."

"And you didn't think to tell anyone else?" he pressed. "Not Sareth? Not another member of the council?"

Elyra's jaw tightened. "I didn't think I needed to. I thought you trusted me."

Rhyven flinched, his arms lowering slightly. For a moment, the fire in his eyes flickered, and Elyra thought she saw something else—something like regret. But it vanished as quickly as it appeared.

"This isn't about trust," he said, his tone more measured now. "It's about the choices we make. You know as well as I do that the rebellion is circling like a pack of wolves. You know I need every ally I have. And yet you risk yourself—"

"I didn't mean to," Elyra interrupted. "I never meant to put myself in danger. I thought I was doing what was right."

"And what if you'd died?" he said, his voice dropping to a near whisper. "What then, Elyra?"

She had no answer. The question hung in the air, heavy and unyielding. She didn't know what would have happened if she'd died, if the assassin's blade had found its mark. Would Rhyven have carried on without her? Would the rebellion have claimed the palace? Would the curse have run its course, unchallenged and unchecked?

The silence stretched between them, and with it came a distance that hadn't been there before. Elyra could feel it growing, like a rift cutting through the ground beneath her feet. Rhyven turned away from her, his hand running through his dark hair as he stepped closer to the fireplace.

"I can't do this alone," he said, more to himself than to her. "I can't fight a rebellion, break a curse, and protect everyone at once."

Elyra took a step toward him. "You don't have to do it alone. I'm here. I've always been here."

He turned his head slightly, just enough to glance at her out of the corner of his eye. "Then stop acting like you're on your own. I need you, Elyra. But not like this. Not if you're going to throw yourself into danger without thinking."

Her breath caught in her throat. His words were raw, unguarded. He wasn't the king in that moment. He wasn't the warrior. He was just a man standing on the edge of a precipice, reaching out for something—someone—to steady him.

"I won't do it again," she said softly. "I'll be more careful."

Rhyven turned fully to face her, his expression still guarded, but his posture less rigid. "We can't afford any more mistakes. If you have information, come to me. If you hear something, tell me. But don't put yourself at risk again."

Elyra nodded, her throat tightening. "I won't."

For a moment, the tension between them seemed to ease, the rift narrowing slightly. But it wasn't gone. The wound was still there, the scar not yet formed. Rhyven's gaze lingered on her for a heartbeat longer before he stepped past her, toward the door.

"I'll have the guards doubled," he said over his shoulder. "And

I'll look into this Seron. If he's tied to the council, we'll find him."

Elyra nodded again, her hands clasping together tightly. "Good."

Rhyven paused at the door, his hand resting on the handle. He turned back, his expression unreadable. "Thank you for the warning. Just… next time, don't come alone."

"I understand," Elyra said quietly.

He opened the door and stepped out, leaving her standing in the dim room. The air felt colder now, the silence even heavier. Elyra stared at the door long after it had closed, her mind a whirlwind of thoughts.

She had come to warn him, to help him. And yet, she had only managed to widen the distance between them. The trust they had built over years of service and prophecy now felt fragile, tenuous. Her own guilt pressed down on her—guilt not just for putting herself in danger, but for the greater betrayal she had not yet confessed.

The rift between them was not just about this night. It was about the secrets she kept, the truths she hadn't told. And as she stood there, alone in the cold chamber, Elyra realized that the rift might never close. Not until the truth came to light.

The Unraveling Curse

The air was heavy with the weight of unseen forces, a suffocating tension that hung in the corridors of the ancient palace. Elyra moved through the halls with purpose, her white robes whispering against the cold stone floor. Her steps were deliberate, yet the unease clawing at her chest made her falter once or twice. She was being watched—of that she was certain.

For days now, the visions had come more frequently, and with each one, the curse that bound Rhyven seemed to grow more volatile. What once had been a shadow at the edge of her sight had now become a storm raging in her mind's eye. She had seen fragments—flashes of bloodied steel, the shattered sigil of the crown, and Rhyven himself on his knees, his strength drained, his golden eyes dull with despair.

The corridors twisted, the flickering torchlight casting eerie shadows. Elyra clutched the small leather pouch at her side, its contents heavier than they should have been. The ancient tokens within were meant to help her focus, to summon the visions at her will rather than be a passive vessel. It was a dangerous act, attempting to control the flow of fate, but there was no other choice. The curse was accelerating. If she didn't act soon, the rebellion would be the least of their worries.

At last, she reached the sealed chamber—the heart of the temple archives, where the oldest texts and relics of Kharoth were kept. The door bore the mark of the Oracle's lineage, a sigil older than the kingdom itself. Elyra pressed her hand to the carved emblem, muttering a phrase in the old tongue. The door groaned as the magic within recognized her, unlocking with a heavy click.

Inside, the room was cold, the air stale from centuries of disuse. Scrolls and tomes lined the walls, their spines cracked with age. A single brazier burned in the center, casting flickering light over the runes carved into the floor. It was here, in this sacred place, that Elyra would attempt to unravel the curse that had bound Rhyven since his birth.

She knelt before the brazier, her fingers trembling as she laid out the items from her pouch—a shard of blackened glass, a coil of silver wire, a drop of her own blood sealed in a crystal vial. These were the keys, the ancient artifacts that would allow her to trace the curse back to its source.

Closing her eyes, she whispered the incantation.

The chamber darkened. The fire in the brazier flared, the shadows on the walls twisting into shapes that no longer resembled the room's features. Elyra's breathing slowed as her mind plunged into the void, the boundaries of the physical world melting away.

And then, the visions began.

She saw the throne room, but not as it was now. The tapestries were different, the crest of the kingdom not yet tarnished by war. Rhyven's father stood before the ancient altar, a younger man than she remembered from the history books. Beside him, a figure cloaked in shadows whispered in his ear. The words were not audible, but the intent was clear—power, protection, dominion over all enemies.

The king knelt before the altar, cutting his palm with a ceremonial dagger. His blood spilled onto the stone, and the runes on the floor ignited with a crimson glow. The cloaked figure raised a hand, their voice echoing in an otherworldly tongue. The scene shifted violently.

Elyra now saw the royal nursery. A young boy, no more than three years old, sat on the floor, playing with a wooden soldier. A nursemaid watched him from the corner, her face drawn with worry. And then, the shadows crept in. The boy—the young Rhyven—did not notice as a black mist seeped through the cracks of the walls. It coiled around him, unseen by the nursemaid, wrapping him in tendrils of darkness. The curse was no longer dormant.

Elyra tried to reach out, her mind pushing against the vision. She needed to know more. Who had cast the curse? What was its true purpose? The images blurred, her own voice ringing out in the chamber as she demanded answers from the shadows.

The scene changed again. She was no longer in the palace. She stood in a barren landscape, a void where the sky and ground were indistinguishable. A figure emerged—tall, cloaked, their face obscured by a silver mask. This was the source. The one who had bound Rhyven to his fate.

"Who are you?" Elyra's voice echoed, the sound swallowed by the endless expanse.

The figure tilted its head, as if amused. When it spoke, its voice was both ancient and terrible, a chorus of whispers overlapping into a single sound. "I am the keeper of the debt. The one who ensures the bargain is fulfilled."

"What bargain?" Elyra pressed, her heart pounding.

"The bloodline was spared annihilation. The kingdom was given strength. And in return, the firstborn heir would bear the weight of the curse." The figure stepped closer, the silver mask glinting faintly in the shadowless light. "The cost cannot be undone. It must be paid."

Elyra clenched her fists, her voice rising. "There has to be another way. Tell me how to break it."

The figure stopped, its presence overwhelming. "To unravel

the curse is to undo the bargain. And to undo the bargain…" The mask seemed to smile, though it had no mouth. "Would bring ruin greater than you can imagine."

The vision snapped away like a thread breaking under tension. Elyra was back in the chamber, gasping for breath. The brazier's flames had dwindled, leaving the room dim and cold. Her hands trembled as she grasped the edge of the stone altar for support.

She had seen it. The bargain that had been made. The cost that had been set. And the consequences that would follow if she unraveled it.

Rhyven's fate was tied not only to the curse, but to the kingdom's very foundation. If she broke it, the kingdom could fall. If she left it, Rhyven would die.

Elyra sank to her knees, the enormity of the truth crashing down upon her. For the first time, she felt truly powerless. The threads of fate were knotted beyond her ability to untangle, and the path forward was shrouded in darkness.

Fourteen

Betrayal in the Court

The tension in the great hall was palpable, a quiet storm crackling through the air. Elyra stood behind one of the stone pillars, hidden from view as the royal council gathered. She wasn't supposed to be here. The Oracle was called into court only when her visions were formally requested. But tonight, she had come unbidden, drawn by the whispers of rebellion that had infiltrated the palace like poison.

The chamber was dimly lit, the flickering torchlight casting jagged shadows across the stone walls. Around the long oak table, the high lords of Kharoth were seated, their faces etched with worry, suspicion, and ambition. At the head of the table sat Rhyven, his golden eyes scanning the room, his presence a looming force even as the discussions turned increasingly heated.

Elyra pressed herself against the cool stone, her pulse quickening. The murmurs of treachery she had heard over the past days were no longer vague. There were names now, faces hidden behind masks of loyalty. She had tried to warn Rhyven, but he had been too consumed by the rebellion at the borders, the curse that haunted him, and the pressure of holding the kingdom together.

"My king," a voice rose above the low rumble of conversation. Lord Verran, a man whose cunning was matched only by his influence, stood with a slight bow. His dark eyes gleamed in the torchlight, and his voice carried a faint, silken edge. "We cannot continue this war without further resources. The rebellion has drained our coffers, and the people are growing restless. We must consider… alternative alliances."

Rhyven's gaze was sharp. "You would suggest a truce with traitors?"

"Not a truce, my king," Verran replied, his tone smooth. "An understanding. If we can isolate the most influential factions within the rebellion and bring them to the negotiating table, we can buy ourselves time. Time to strengthen our defenses, to—"

"To show weakness," another voice interrupted, Lord Tyrian. He was older, his beard streaked with gray, his scarred face a testament to his years of service on the battlefield. "What you're proposing is surrender by another name. If the king were to negotiate with these rebels, it would undermine the very foundation of his rule."

Verran smiled faintly, a serpentine curve of the lips. "You misunderstand me, Lord Tyrian. I am not advocating for surrender. I am merely suggesting a tactical approach—"

"Enough," Rhyven said, his voice cutting through the room like a blade. The lords fell silent, their eyes shifting to the king. Rhyven leaned forward, his hands resting on the table. "I will not bargain with traitors. Nor will I cower behind false alliances. This rebellion will be crushed, and those who dare to defy the crown will face the consequences."

Elyra's chest tightened as she watched the exchange. The tension in the room wasn't just about strategy. It was personal. Verran's suggestion, while cloaked in reason, carried a dangerous undertone. And Tyrian's fierce loyalty, though admirable, could easily blind him to subtler threats. The court was fracturing, and somewhere within these walls, betrayal had already taken root.

She shifted slightly, trying to see more clearly, when she heard it—a faint rustle, a barely audible shuffle of movement. Elyra froze, her hand gripping the edge of the pillar. Someone was nearby, someone who shouldn't be. Her instincts screamed at her to stay hidden, but curiosity and a gnawing sense of urgency drove her to glance around the corner.

In the shadows near the rear of the chamber, she caught a glimpse of a figure. They were cloaked, their features obscured, but their posture and the way they hovered near the council's private entrance made her pulse race. This wasn't a servant or a guard. This was someone watching, listening, waiting.

The council's discussion continued, growing more heated as the lords argued over resources, troop movements, and the growing unrest in the city. Rhyven's patience was thinning, but he maintained his composure, his authority unshaken. Yet Elyra's attention remained fixed on the shadowy figure. Every instinct told her that this was the traitor—one of the whispers she had heard, now given form.

She had to act. Quietly, carefully, she slipped away from the pillar, her steps silent against the stone. If she could get closer, if she could see who it was, she could bring the information to Rhyven before it was too late. Her heart pounded as she moved toward the far corner of the chamber, her gaze locked on the figure.

But as she approached, the figure turned abruptly, their head snapping toward her as if sensing her presence. Elyra froze, her breath catching. For a brief moment, their eyes met—a flash of recognition, of awareness. The figure stepped back, melting into the shadows. Elyra moved quickly, but by the time she reached the spot where they had stood, they were gone. The door to the council's private chambers creaked faintly, signaling their retreat.

She stood there, her hands trembling. The traitor had been within reach, but now they had slipped away. And worse, they had seen her.

"Oracle?"

Elyra spun around to find Sareth standing behind her, his

expression a mix of concern and confusion. "What are you doing here?" he asked, his voice low. "You know the council's meetings are closed."

"I…" She hesitated, her mind racing. Should she tell him about the figure she had seen? Would he believe her? Or would he think she was overstepping her bounds? "I needed to speak with the king. It's urgent."

Sareth frowned, glancing toward the council chamber. "They're in the middle of a critical discussion. If it's truly urgent, you'll need to wait until—"

"It can't wait," she interrupted. "There's someone in the palace, someone who doesn't belong. I just saw them—here, in the shadows."

Sareth's expression darkened. "Did you recognize them?"

"No, but they knew I was watching. And they fled as soon as I got close." She stepped closer, lowering her voice. "Sareth, we have to find them. If they're tied to the rebellion—"

"Calm yourself," he said, his tone firm but not unkind. "I'll alert the guards and have the entrances secured. But if there's a traitor in the palace, we can't act hastily. We need proof."

Elyra nodded, though her nerves were still on edge. She watched as Sareth stepped into the shadows, issuing quiet orders to the nearest sentries. The sense of danger remained, a lingering presence that refused to fade.

As she turned back toward the council chamber, her gaze fell on Rhyven. He was still seated at the head of the table, his expression cold and unyielding as the lords bickered around him. He looked every inch the king, a figure of unshakable authority. But Elyra knew better. Beneath that composed exterior was a man burdened by the weight of a kingdom on the brink of collapse.

And now, there was a traitor among them. One who had escaped into the shadows, their motives unknown, their actions shrouded in secrecy. Elyra felt a chill run down her spine. She couldn't tell Rhyven yet—there was too much uncertainty, too many unanswered questions. But she knew one thing for certain: the betrayal within the court was deeper than she had ever imagined, and the fight to uncover the truth had only just begun.

Fifteen

The Hidden Heir

The air in the palace had grown heavier in the days following the council meeting. Tension hung in every corridor, whispered in every corner. Guards tightened their patrols, and the once-lively courtyards were now subdued, the residents exchanging wary glances as they passed. Elyra could feel the shift as keenly as she could feel the chill in the stone walls.

She spent her days delving into the archives and her nights piecing together fragments of visions, trying to unravel the threads that tied the curse, the rebellion, and the shadow council into one tangled knot. But no matter how many tomes she studied, how many hours she spent meditating on the runes etched into the ancient altar, the answers remained elusive.

Until the vision came.

It was not like the others. It came without warning, without ceremony. Elyra was not kneeling before the altar or clutching the silver tokens. She was simply standing in her chamber, staring out the narrow window, when the air around her seemed to shift. The world blurred, and she found herself in a place she had never seen before.

A grand hall, lit by soft golden light. High, arched ceilings adorned with intricate frescoes depicting scenes of a forgotten age. In the center of the hall, a figure stood alone. A man, tall and cloaked, his back turned to her. She couldn't see his face, but the weight of his presence pressed on her like the hand of the gods.

He turned slowly, his features shrouded in shadow. His voice, when he spoke, was deep and resonant. "You seek the truth."

Elyra tried to reply, but no words came. She could only nod.

The man gestured toward the far end of the hall, where a grand throne stood atop a dais. Its surface gleamed with gold and silver, and upon it rested a single object: a small, intricately carved box.

"In there," he said, his voice echoing. "What you seek is within."

Elyra stepped forward, drawn to the box by a force she could not resist. The air grew warmer as she approached, and her hand trembled as she reached out to touch it. The moment her fingers brushed the surface, the vision shattered.

She gasped, staggering back into the cold reality of her chamber. Her heart pounded, and her breath came in short, shallow bursts. The image of the box lingered in her mind, its ornate carvings burned into her memory.

The vision was clear: somewhere within the palace lay a hidden truth, locked away for decades. And now, more than ever, Elyra felt the pull to find it.

It was the dead of night when Elyra left her chambers, her

movements as silent as the shadows that clung to the walls. The corridors were empty, the guards stationed farther away on the upper floors. She had learned from her previous mistakes; she carried no torch, made no sound. The vision had shown her the way—through the main hall, past the council chamber, to a forgotten wing of the palace that even the servants rarely entered.

The door at the end of the corridor was unremarkable, its wooden surface worn smooth with age. But as Elyra approached, she felt a pulse of energy, faint but distinct. This was the place.

She pressed her hand against the door and whispered a single word in the old tongue. The lock clicked, and the door creaked open. Inside was a chamber that hadn't been touched in decades. Dust coated the furniture, and cobwebs stretched between the beams. But in the center of the room, just as she had seen in her vision, stood a dais. And upon it rested the box.

Elyra's breath caught as she stepped closer. The carvings were exactly as she remembered, intricate patterns that seemed to shift and shimmer under the moonlight filtering through a small window. The box was sealed with a simple latch, and as she reached out, her fingers hesitated.

What would she find inside? Another piece of the curse's puzzle? A weapon to be used against the rebellion? Or something worse—something that could not be undone?

With a deep breath, she flipped the latch and opened the box.

Inside, nestled among faded silk, was a single document. Its edges were brittle, its ink faded. Elyra lifted it carefully, holding it up to the moonlight. The words were written in the old tongue, but she could read them well enough.

What she saw made her stomach drop.

The document was a decree, signed and sealed by Rhyven's father, King Varyon. It named a child—a son—born outside of wedlock, hidden away to protect the throne's legitimacy. The child's existence had been erased from the records, his name never spoken in the court. But here it was, etched in ink that refused to fade entirely, a truth buried deep in the palace's heart.

Rhyven had a brother.

Elyra's mind raced. If this was true, then the curse's grip on Rhyven's bloodline was even more complex than she'd feared. The rebellion wasn't just about power or politics—it was tied to the forgotten heir, to the legacy of a king who had made deals in shadows.

And the shadow council knew. They had to know. They had used this secret to sow division, to turn lords against Rhyven, to whisper of another who might take the throne. This was the leverage they had been wielding, the reason for the growing discontent among the nobles.

Elyra placed the document back into the box, her hands trembling. She had found the truth. But what would she do with it?

When Rhyven entered the council chamber the next morning, Elyra was already there. She had asked Sareth to summon him privately, away from the prying eyes and ears of the court. He arrived with his usual commanding presence, his golden eyes locking onto hers the moment he entered the room.

"What is this about?" he asked, his tone sharp.

Elyra took a deep breath and held up the document. "This."

Rhyven frowned, stepping closer. He took the paper from her hand, his gaze scanning the faded text. As he read, his expression darkened. The tension in the room grew thick as he reached the end, his jaw clenching.

"Where did you find this?" he demanded.

"In a forgotten wing of the palace," Elyra said. "It was hidden away, locked and buried."

Rhyven's grip on the document tightened. "And you're certain it's real?"

Elyra nodded. "I've seen enough forgeries to know the difference. This is real."

For a long moment, Rhyven said nothing. He stared down at the paper, his golden eyes blazing with a mix of anger and something else—something more vulnerable, more human. Finally, he set the document down on the table.

"If this is true," he said, his voice low, "then the rebellion may have more than just soldiers and gold. They may have a claim."

"That's what they're counting on," Elyra said quietly. "They're using this secret to turn your allies against you. They believe this hidden heir is their weapon."

Rhyven exhaled sharply, his hand running through his dark hair. "This changes everything."

Elyra stepped closer, her voice steady. "It doesn't change who you are. It doesn't change what you've built, what you've fought for. But it does mean we need to act quickly. The shadow council won't wait. They'll use this revelation to weaken you further."

Rhyven turned to her, his gaze piercing. "Then we'll stop them before they can."

The room was silent as the weight of their discovery settled over them. Elyra knew that the path ahead had grown even more treacherous. But she also knew that they could not turn back. The truth was out, and with it came a new fight—one that would test the strength of the throne, the loyalty of the kingdom, and the resolve of a king who had always carried more than his share of burdens.

Sixteen

A Heart Bound by Magic

The sun sank low over Kharoth, painting the palace walls in hues of molten gold and crimson. Elyra moved through the quiet corridors, the distant murmur of servants barely reaching her ears. In her hands, she clutched the fragment of parchment she had retrieved from the ancient box, its words still burning in her mind. Every step brought her closer to a truth she wasn't ready to face, yet she could not turn back now.

She stopped before a heavy wooden door adorned with a carved sigil—an eye encircled by flames. The Chamber of Illumination, a room reserved for the Oracle's most sacred rituals, where the boundary between the mortal world and the divine grew thin. It was here that she would finally confront the magic binding Rhyven's fate. The answers had eluded her for too long, and the visions were growing more chaotic, more intense. Time was running out.

Elyra whispered the incantation that unsealed the door, her voice steady despite the storm within her. The locks clicked softly, and she pushed the door open. The chamber beyond was dimly lit, the only illumination coming from a ring of candles surrounding the central altar. The air was thick with the scent of aged parchment, molten wax, and something darker—something that lingered at the edge of her senses, a faint hum that vibrated in her bones.

She stepped inside, closing the door behind her. The chamber felt alive, as though it had been waiting for her. The flames of the candles flickered unnaturally, their movements too deliberate, too synchronized. Elyra's fingers tightened around the parchment as she approached the altar. On its surface lay an ancient tome, its leather cover cracked with age and its edges singed as if it had once been consumed by fire but refused to burn.

Elyra set the parchment down beside the tome and hesitated. This was no simple spell she sought to unravel. The curse on Rhyven's bloodline was not just a binding of words or symbols; it was a living thing, coiled around his very essence. She had seen it in her visions, felt its cold tendrils reaching out to her whenever she tried to peer into its origins. To confront it directly was to risk her own mind, her own soul. But what choice did she have?

She opened the tome, the brittle pages crackling softly. The language was one she had studied for years, a dialect of the old tongue reserved for the most dangerous and forbidden magics. She traced the runes on the page, her breath slowing as she began to read.

The Binding of the First Heir, the title read, the words etched deep into the page as though they had been carved rather than written. Below it, the text described a ritual performed at the moment of a child's birth. Blood from the parent, blood from the newborn, and a single strand of hair from the one who carried the curse's will. These elements were combined in a vessel of black stone, then sealed with a glyph that could only be spoken by the one who cast it. The result was a curse that could not be broken through conventional means. It was designed to endure until the conditions of the original bargain were met.

Elyra's stomach churned as she read further. The curse was more than a mere spell—it was a pact. Rhyven's father had traded his firstborn son's life to ensure the kingdom's survival, to protect it from an external threat that even now remained unnamed. The rebellion was not the cause of the curse but a symptom, a consequence of the imbalance created by the bargain. The shadow council's actions were a direct response to that ancient magic, a rebellion born of a kingdom bound by an unbreakable chain.

Her fingers trembled as she turned the page. The text detailed the effects of the curse, how it would manifest as the heir grew older. The child would be marked by strength and resilience, surviving wounds that would kill ordinary men, rising again from illnesses that should claim their life. But this strength was not a blessing—it was the curse's hold, ensuring that the heir would endure until the precise moment their life was demanded as payment. The very heart of the heir would become a vessel, a source of magic that kept the kingdom stable. And when that heart stopped beating, the magic would be released, and the kingdom's foundations would tremble.

Elyra's breath hitched. This was the reason Rhyven could not simply flee, could not simply ignore his fate. His very existence was tied to the kingdom's survival. If he fell, the land itself would suffer. The rebellion's leaders knew this. They sought to exploit it, to trigger the release of the curse's power and reshape the kingdom to their will.

She turned another page, and her gaze fell upon a single, haunting line:

To sever the bond, the heart must be claimed by the one who bound it.

Elyra froze. The words were simple, yet their meaning cut through her like a blade. The one who had cast the curse—the shadowy figure she had glimpsed in her visions—still held the key. If that person could be found, if they could be confronted, perhaps the curse could be unmade. But the text gave no clue as to who this figure was, only that they had acted as an intermediary, a conduit through which the bargain was sealed.

The candles flickered violently, the flames rising high before settling again. The air in the chamber grew colder, and Elyra felt a chill creep up her spine. She was not alone.

Her hand drifted toward the small dagger at her belt, more a token of protection than a true weapon. She turned slowly, her eyes scanning the shadows. The chamber was still, yet the sense of another presence remained. It wasn't the shadow council or one of their spies. This presence was different—ancient, patient, and watchful.

"Who's there?" she demanded, her voice steady despite the fear coiling in her chest.

The air shifted, a faint whisper brushing against her ear. It was not a voice, not words, but a feeling—a warning. Elyra's grip on the dagger tightened as she took a step back toward the altar. Whatever was in the chamber with her, it did not move closer. It lingered at the edges, as if testing her resolve.

She turned back to the tome, her heart pounding. The answer was here. It had to be. She skimmed the text, searching for anything that could tell her how to find the one who had cast the curse. Her eyes landed on another line:

The blood that binds, the blood that betrays, the blood that breaks.

The words made no immediate sense, but Elyra committed them to memory. She closed the tome and tucked the parchment into her robe. She had what she needed for now— knowledge, however incomplete, and a direction to pursue.

As she stepped out of the chamber, the air felt lighter, as though whatever had been watching her had withdrawn. She locked the door behind her, her fingers lingering on the cool wood. The path ahead was clear but fraught with danger. To break the curse, she would need to confront the one who had cast it. And to do that, she would have to walk deeper into the shadows than ever before.

Seventeen

The Battle for the Throne

The gates of the palace shuddered under the weight of the first battering ram. Rhyven stood on the battlements, his golden eyes narrowed against the morning sun as he surveyed the battlefield below. The shadow council's forces had come sooner than anticipated, their banners dark against the rising light. Columns of soldiers surged toward the main gate, their ranks bristling with spears and shields. Above them, archers rained down volleys of arrows that shimmered in the sunlight like silver needles.

Behind him, the courtyard swarmed with activity. Runners darted back and forth, carrying orders, while soldiers lined the walls with crossbows and boiling oil. The air smelled of smoke and sweat, a sharp contrast to the calm that had blanketed the city just a few days prior.

"Your Majesty," Sareth called, climbing the narrow staircase to join him. The general's face was set in a grim mask, his armor dented and scratched from the morning's skirmishes. "The eastern wall won't hold much longer. If they breach the gate before our reinforcements arrive, we'll lose control of the courtyard."

Rhyven's jaw tightened, his hand resting on the hilt of his sword. "Then we'll make our stand here. We cannot let them reach the throne room."

Below, the battering ram struck again, the iron-tipped log splintering the wood of the great gates. A resounding crack echoed through the palace grounds, and Rhyven knew it was only a matter of time.

"Signal the reserves," he ordered, his voice calm despite the chaos. "Tell them to reinforce the eastern wall. If we lose the courtyard, we'll make our stand in the throne room itself."

Sareth hesitated for only a moment before nodding. "As you command." He turned and descended the stairs, barking orders as he went.

Rhyven drew his sword, the blade gleaming as if it hungered for the fight ahead. The battle was not just for the city or the palace. It was for the throne itself—the heart of Kharoth's power. If the shadow council claimed it, they wouldn't just take the crown; they would take the soul of the kingdom.

—-

Elyra pressed herself against the cool stone of the palace walls, her heart pounding in her chest. She had taken the secret passage from the Oracle's chambers to the main hall, her mind racing as she tried to piece together what she had learned. The curse, the shadow council, the rebellion—they were all threads in the same dark tapestry.

The visions had shown her the shadow council's plans in fragmented glimpses: soldiers storming the throne room, the crown cast to the floor, and a figure cloaked in darkness sitting upon the throne. But they had also shown her something else, something she had not yet dared to voice. A figure standing behind Rhyven, blade in hand.

A traitor.

And the traitor was close.

Elyra hurried down the narrow corridor, her robes catching on the rough stone as the sound of battle grew louder. She had to find Rhyven, to warn him before it was too late. The throne room was still secure for now, but the defenses were crumbling. The eastern wall had already fallen, and the shadow council's forces were pouring in like a flood.

As she rounded the corner, she nearly collided with Sareth. The general caught her arm, his expression a mix of surprise and frustration.

"What are you doing here?" he demanded, his voice low but urgent. "You should be in the sanctum, not wandering the halls."

"I have to see the king," Elyra said, her voice trembling with urgency. "It's important."

"Important enough to risk your life?" he asked, his eyes narrowing. "You don't belong on the battlefield, Oracle."

"This isn't just a battle," she shot back. "There's something else—someone else. The shadow council isn't working alone."

Sareth's grip tightened on her arm. "What do you mean?"

"There's a traitor," she said, the words rushing out. "Someone close to the king. I saw it in the visions."

Sareth's jaw clenched, his gaze hardening. "Who?"

Elyra hesitated. The face in the vision had been obscured, the figure shrouded in shadows. She didn't know who the traitor was, only that they were in the palace, close enough to strike.

"I don't know," she admitted, her voice barely above a whisper.

Sareth's expression darkened. "Then stay here," he ordered. "I'll warn the king."

"No!" Elyra grabbed his arm before he could leave. "I have to tell him myself. He needs to hear it from me."

Sareth looked at her for a long moment before nodding reluctantly. "Then stay close. And don't do anything foolish."

—-

The throne room doors loomed ahead, their ornate carvings glowing faintly in the torchlight. The sounds of battle were louder now—shouts, the clash of steel, and the distant thunder of another battering ram striking the main gate. Elyra followed Sareth as he pushed open the heavy doors, revealing the grand hall within.

Rhyven stood at the far end, his sword drawn, his golden eyes scanning the room. His presence was commanding, his expression calm despite the chaos outside. Around him, a small group of loyal soldiers formed a defensive line, their shields raised, their spears ready.

Sareth approached quickly, his voice low as he relayed the situation. Elyra hung back, her eyes darting around the room. She felt it again—that prickling sensation at the back of her neck, the faint hum of magic in the air.

The traitor was here.

Rhyven's voice broke through her thoughts. "The eastern wall is lost?"

"Yes, Your Majesty," Sareth replied. "The reserves are holding them off for now, but we need to be ready for a breach."

Rhyven nodded, his grip on his sword tightening. "Then we hold the throne room. We don't retreat any further."

Elyra stepped forward, her voice trembling but firm. "Your Majesty, there's something you need to know."

Rhyven turned to her, his expression unreadable. "Speak quickly, Oracle."

"There's a traitor," she said, her heart pounding. "Someone inside the palace, someone close to you. I've seen it."

The soldiers exchanged uneasy glances, and Sareth's hand drifted toward his sword hilt. Rhyven's gaze remained locked on Elyra.

"Who?" he asked, his voice sharp.

"I don't know," she admitted, her chest tightening. "But they're here. They're waiting for the right moment."

Rhyven's eyes narrowed, and he took a step toward her. "Are you certain of this?"

"Yes," Elyra said, her voice steady. "I saw it in the visions. The shadow council isn't acting alone."

Before Rhyven could respond, the throne room doors shuddered. The sound of splintering wood echoed through the hall, followed by the cries of soldiers outside. The shadow council's forces were at the gates.

Rhyven turned to his men, his voice rising. "Hold the line! No one passes through these doors."

The soldiers snapped to attention, forming a tight formation near the entrance. Sareth drew his sword, positioning himself near the king.

Elyra's pulse quickened as the traitor's presence grew stronger. She couldn't see them, but she could feel them—an oppressive force waiting to strike. Her gaze darted from face to face, searching for any sign of betrayal.

And then it happened.

A soldier, one of Rhyven's own guards, stepped forward. His movement was swift, almost too fast to follow. His blade gleamed in the torchlight as he turned, not toward the enemy, but toward the king.

"Rhyven!" Elyra screamed.

The king reacted instantly, his sword meeting the traitor's strike with a resounding clash. The hall erupted into chaos as the other soldiers moved to subdue the attacker, but the traitor fought with a ferocity that spoke of dark purpose.

Elyra watched, her heart in her throat, as Rhyven parried blow after blow. The traitor's face twisted with rage, his eyes burning with something unnatural. This was no ordinary betrayal. This was the shadow council's hand at work, the curse itself pushing its pawn to strike at the heart of the kingdom.

In that moment, the battle for the throne was no longer just about steel and blood. It was a battle against the darkness that sought to claim them all.

Eighteen

The Oracle's Choice

Elyra stood frozen as the hall descended into chaos. The clash of steel against steel rang out like thunder, and the once-majestic throne room transformed into a battlefield. Rhyven's blade met the traitor's with a resounding strike, the force sending sparks into the air. Around them, the loyal guards fought to push back the encroaching soldiers, their shouts lost beneath the din of the fray.

She gripped the edge of a stone column, her mind racing. The visions that had plagued her for days had warned her of this moment, but they hadn't told her how to stop it. All she had seen was the blood, the betrayal, and the heart-wrenching decision that lay ahead.

Rhyven fought like a man possessed, each swing of his sword deliberate and powerful. The traitor—a guard who had been by his side for years—moved with an unnatural ferocity. There was no hesitation in his attacks, no flicker of remorse in his eyes. It was as if something dark and ancient had taken hold, driving him to strike at the very man he had once sworn to protect.

"Hold the line!" Rhyven bellowed, his voice cutting through the chaos. His men rallied, forming a tighter defensive circle around the throne. But Elyra could see the strain in their faces, the doubt creeping in as the enemy pushed closer.

Her hand drifted to the small vial hanging from her belt. It was a relic she had carried for years, a last resort that she had never dared to use. Inside was a single drop of enchanted blood, a fragment of the curse that bound Rhyven's bloodline. The tome she had studied warned of the vial's power, of the dire consequences of unleashing it. But in this moment, with the throne room on the verge of falling, Elyra felt the weight of her responsibility pressing down on her.

If she used it, the traitor would be stopped. The immediate threat would end, and Rhyven's life would be spared—at least for now. But the cost...

Elyra's chest tightened. The visions had shown her that the curse was not simply an affliction. It was a bond, a tether that held the kingdom together in ways no one fully understood. To disrupt it, to tamper with its essence, could unravel everything. The kingdom's stability, its very foundation, was tied to the bloodline's magic. If she unleashed the vial's power, the balance could tip into chaos.

A guard cried out nearby, his body crumpling under the weight of an enemy's blade. Elyra flinched, her breath quickening. The choice was hers to make. Stand by and let fate run its course, or intervene and risk everything she had worked to protect.

Her gaze fell on Rhyven. His golden eyes burned with determination, his every move a testament to his strength and resolve. He fought for his kingdom, for his people. But even he could not see the full scope of what was at stake. He didn't know what the curse truly meant, nor the dangers of disrupting it.

The traitor lunged again, and Rhyven parried just in time. The traitor's blade scraped against his armor, a near-fatal blow narrowly avoided. Elyra's grip on the vial tightened. The weight of the choice crushed her, and she felt the cold stone at her back as if it were the only thing keeping her standing.

And then, as if summoned by her turmoil, a voice whispered through her mind—a voice that wasn't her own.

You know what must be done.

Elyra's heart stopped. The voice was ancient, distant, yet clear as day. It resonated within her, a reminder of the power she had been entrusted with. The Oracle was not merely a guide, not merely a seer. She was a conduit, a vessel for forces far older than the kingdom itself.

Her hand trembled as she uncorked the vial. The liquid inside shimmered, a crimson drop suspended in an unnatural stillness. The air around her seemed to shift, growing colder, heavier.

The moment she released the blood's power, there would be no turning back.

But she had no other option. The traitor's blade rose again, poised to strike at the king. Time slowed, each second stretching into an eternity. Elyra stepped forward, holding the vial aloft. Her voice rang out, steady and clear despite the chaos.

"By the blood that binds us, by the power that holds this kingdom, I call upon the ancient pact. Release the shadow's grasp and bring balance to the throne!"

The vial's contents shimmered brighter, and then, with a sound like a thousand whispers rising at once, the liquid evaporated. A wave of force rippled through the room, knocking friend and foe alike to the ground. The traitor froze mid-strike, his blade suspended in the air. For a moment, the room was silent.

And then the traitor screamed.

It was a sound unlike anything Elyra had ever heard, a raw, guttural cry that echoed through the stone walls. The shadows that had clung to him, that had driven him, began to unravel. Black tendrils of magic writhed and hissed, dissipating into the air like smoke caught in a gale. The traitor's body convulsed, and then he collapsed, the sword clattering to the ground beside him.

Rhyven staggered back, his chest heaving as he caught his breath. His gaze shot to Elyra, and for a moment, their eyes met. The question in his golden eyes was clear: What have you done?

The answer was more complicated than she could explain.

The guards slowly began to rise, their confusion evident. The shadow council's forces hesitated, as if sensing that something had shifted. The tide of battle stalled, the momentum disrupted by the sudden surge of magic.

Elyra lowered her hand, her chest tight. She had saved Rhyven, saved the throne. But at what cost?

As the dust settled, she felt the weight of the choice she had made. The curse's grip had been loosened, but it was not gone. The kingdom was still bound by ancient magic, still tethered to forces that few could comprehend. And Elyra knew that she had only bought them time—time to uncover the truth, to find a way to truly break the curse without shattering the kingdom in the process.

Rhyven approached her, his expression guarded. He stood before her, his sword still in hand, his gaze piercing. "What did you do?" he asked, his voice low.

"I saved you," she said softly.

"At what cost?" he demanded.

Elyra swallowed hard. "I don't know. But I couldn't let you die."

The room was still, the weight of her words settling over them. Rhyven's jaw tightened, but he nodded. "We'll face that cost together, then. Whatever it may be."

She nodded, though a part of her doubted the path she had set them on. The choice had been hers alone, but the consequences would be shared by all.

As the battle outside the throne room slowly resumed, Elyra felt the weight of her decision press down on her like never before. The Oracle's choice had been made, but the full extent of its impact was still to come.

Nineteen

The Death of Fate

The storm rolled over the horizon, casting an unnatural shadow across the battlefield. Black clouds churned violently, flashes of lightning illuminating the chaos below. The clash of steel and the cries of soldiers filled the air, a symphony of destruction that seemed to grow louder with each passing moment. And at the center of it all, standing alone against the encroaching darkness, was Rhyven.

His golden eyes burned fiercely, his sword gleaming as if it held a fragment of the sun. Blood streaked his armor, his breaths coming in heavy gasps, yet he did not falter. The rebels surged forward like an unending tide, and he met them head-on, his blade cutting through the storm of bodies. Each strike was precise, each movement fueled by an unyielding determination that pushed him beyond exhaustion.

Elyra watched from the edge of the battlefield, her heart pounding in her chest. She had warned him of the cost, of the dangers that lay ahead. The visions had shown her this moment countless times, but standing here now, with the winds whipping around her and the smell of blood in the air, she realized the weight of those visions could never truly prepare her for the reality.

The shadow council's forces pressed closer, their numbers overwhelming. Their leaders had not yet revealed themselves, but Elyra could feel their presence—an oppressive, malevolent force that seemed to twist the very fabric of the world. The curse's influence was no longer subtle. It was manifesting in the storm, in the earth that trembled beneath their feet, in the cries of men whose voices were swallowed by the howling wind.

Elyra's grip tightened around the staff she had taken from the temple's reliquary. Its surface was cool under her fingers, the ancient wood pulsing faintly with magic. She had brought it as a last resort, a tool that could channel her power and give her a fighting chance if the worst came to pass. And now, as she stood on the precipice of fate itself, she felt its weight as both a weapon and a burden.

Rhyven's voice rang out across the battlefield, commanding his troops to hold the line. The soldiers rallied around him, forming a defensive wall against the onslaught. They believed in him, trusted him, even as the darkness pressed closer. But Elyra knew what they did not—that the outcome of this battle had already been written in blood and shadow.

A sudden shift in the storm drew her attention. The clouds above churned more violently, a vortex forming in the sky. The wind howled louder, carrying with it a deep, resonant hum that made the ground vibrate. Elyra's stomach tightened as she realized what was happening. The shadow council's leaders were making their move.

"Rhyven!" she shouted, her voice barely audible above the gale. She ran toward him, her feet slipping on the muddy ground as she fought against the wind. Her robes clung to her skin, soaked through by the driving rain. "They're coming!"

He turned toward her, his eyes locking on hers for a brief moment. He nodded, a silent acknowledgment of her warning, before stepping back into the fray. His sword flashed in the dim light, cutting down another foe as the rebel forces surged forward once more.

Elyra stopped short, her chest heaving. She could see them now—figures emerging from the shadows at the far end of the battlefield. They wore dark, intricately woven robes, their faces obscured by masks that gleamed faintly in the storm's light. They moved with purpose, their hands weaving patterns in the air, and with each gesture, the storm above them grew more ferocious.

It was them. The architects of the rebellion, the ones who had pulled the strings from the start. And they were not just mortal men and women. The magic that surrounded them was ancient, forbidden. They were channeling the curse itself, bending its power to their will.

Elyra's hands tightened on the staff. She had studied the curse, pieced together its origins and its purpose. She knew that it was more than a spell—it was a force of nature, a bond that had been woven into the fabric of the kingdom's existence. To confront it directly was to risk everything. But as she looked out at the battlefield, at Rhyven standing against impossible odds, she knew she had no choice.

The leaders of the shadow council began their chant, their voices rising in unison. The hum that filled the air grew deafening, and the ground beneath Elyra's feet trembled violently. A wave of energy pulsed outward, sending soldiers from both sides sprawling. Rhyven staggered but remained upright, his sword planted firmly in the ground as he braced himself against the force.

"Elyra!" he called out, his voice raw. "What are they doing?"

She stepped forward, the staff crackling with power in her hands. "They're trying to break the curse's seal. If they succeed—"

The ground split open, a jagged fissure snaking its way through the battlefield. Black tendrils of energy surged upward, coiling around the figures of the shadow council's leaders. They raised their hands, and the tendrils lashed out, striking at the soldiers who tried to advance. The rebels fell to their knees, their bodies convulsing as the dark energy consumed them. Even Rhyven's men faltered, their shields raised in vain against the onslaught.

Elyra gritted her teeth, her heart pounding. She had to act now.

She raised the staff, her voice rising above the storm as she spoke the incantation she had memorized from the ancient tome. The runes on the staff glowed brighter, and a shield of light enveloped her. The tendrils of darkness recoiled as she stepped forward, pushing closer to the source of the curse's power.

The shadow council's leaders turned their masked faces toward her. Their chant faltered, and for a moment, the storm seemed to still. The battlefield fell silent except for the crackle of energy in the air. Elyra locked eyes with the tallest figure among them, a towering presence whose mask bore the intricate symbol of the ancient pact.

"You can't stop this," the figure said, their voice deep and resonant. "Fate cannot be undone."

Elyra's grip on the staff tightened. "Fate is not immutable," she replied. "It can be rewritten."

The leader tilted their head, as if considering her words. "And you think you have the power to defy what was written in blood?"

"I think I have no choice."

The figure raised a hand, and the tendrils surged toward her. Elyra thrust the staff forward, the shield of light expanding outward. The darkness collided with the barrier, sparks flying as the two forces clashed. Her arms shook under the strain, her knees threatening to give out, but she held firm.

Behind her, Rhyven fought his way toward her, his golden eyes locked on the leaders of the shadow council. He cut down the last of the rebel soldiers in his path and reached her side, his breathing heavy.

"We end this now," he said, his voice steady despite the chaos around them.

Elyra nodded, her eyes never leaving the shadow council's leader. The storm raged on, the ground quaked, and the air grew thick with energy. The fate of the kingdom hung in the balance, and Elyra knew that one way or another, this battle would decide everything.

Twenty

A Love Beyond Destiny

Elyra's heart pounded as she stood at the edge of the fissure, the yawning chasm that had torn through the battlefield. The storm still raged overhead, clouds roiling and black, streaked with veins of angry red lightning. Rhyven was at her side, his sword drawn, his golden eyes scanning the dark figures ahead. The shadow council's leaders had not moved, their masked faces turned toward the two of them as though waiting. Their silence was more unsettling than any battle cry, their stillness more dangerous than the chaos that surrounded them.

She could feel the power radiating from them, pulsing like a second heartbeat in the air. It wasn't just magic; it was something older, deeper, a force that twisted and coiled around the land itself. The curse that bound Rhyven's bloodline was woven into their presence, and she knew that confronting them meant more than just facing skilled adversaries. This was a confrontation with destiny itself.

"You know they won't stop," Rhyven said quietly, his voice cutting through the din of the storm. "They'll see this through to the end, no matter the cost."

Elyra nodded. "I know."

He turned to her, his expression firm but not unkind. "Then why are you hesitating?"

Her grip on the staff tightened, her knuckles white. "Because I know what it will take to end this."

Rhyven's gaze sharpened. "What do you mean?"

"They're tied to the curse," she said, her voice low and urgent. "They're its keepers, its anchors. If we destroy them, we disrupt the curse's hold on your bloodline. But…"

"But what?"

Elyra hesitated, the words catching in her throat. She had seen the truth in her visions, the price of breaking the curse. It was not just a matter of killing the shadow council's leaders. It was not just about defeating their army or reclaiming the throne. To sever the curse, to truly unbind Rhyven from its grasp, would require a sacrifice that went beyond steel and blood.

"It will change everything," she said at last, her voice barely audible. "Not just for you, but for the kingdom. For the land itself."

Rhyven's jaw tightened. He took a step closer, his presence grounding her even as the storm threatened to tear them apart. "We'll face it together," he said firmly. "Whatever it takes."

Elyra wanted to believe him, wanted to draw strength from his resolve. But the visions had shown her more than just the battle. They had shown her a choice, a moment when she would have to decide not just the fate of the curse, but the fate of her own heart. And now, standing here on the precipice of that moment, she wasn't sure she was strong enough.

A sudden surge of energy rippled through the air. The shadow council's leaders moved as one, raising their arms. Black tendrils of magic erupted from the ground, snaking through the battlefield. Soldiers screamed as the dark energy consumed them, their bodies collapsing like marionettes with their strings cut.

Rhyven raised his sword, stepping in front of Elyra. "Stay behind me," he ordered, his voice steady even as the ground trembled beneath their feet.

"No," Elyra said, her voice firm. "We do this together."

She stepped forward, the staff glowing with a soft, steady light. The runes etched into its surface pulsed in time with her heartbeat, a rhythm that echoed in her ears. She could feel the power building within her, the ancient magic that connected her to the land, to the curse, to Rhyven. It was not just a tool—it was a bond, a thread that tied them together in ways she was only beginning to understand.

The shadow council's leaders moved closer, their forms blurred by the storm. Their chanting grew louder, their voices weaving together into a haunting melody that reverberated in the air. Elyra felt her knees weaken, the pressure of their magic pressing down on her like a physical weight. But she stood firm, drawing on the power of the staff, on the strength of her own will.

"We end this now," she said, her voice carrying over the storm. "No more running, no more hiding."

Rhyven nodded, his grip on his sword tightening. "Then let's finish it."

The two of them moved as one. Rhyven charged forward, his blade cutting through the tendrils of darkness that lashed out at him. Elyra followed close behind, the staff's light pushing back the shadows. The shadow council's leaders raised their hands, their magic surging toward them in a wave of black energy. But Elyra thrust the staff forward, the light expanding in a protective shield that absorbed the attack.

Rhyven reached the first of the shadow council's leaders, his sword meeting their staff with a resounding clash. Sparks flew as the two weapons collided, the force of the impact sending shockwaves through the ground. The masked figure retaliated with a burst of magic, but Rhyven sidestepped, his blade slicing through their defenses.

Elyra focused on the others, the staff glowing brighter as she channeled her power. She spoke the incantation she had memorized, the words resonating in the storm. The runes on the staff pulsed in time with her chant, and the light grew stronger, pushing back the darkness.

The shadow council's leaders faltered. Their chanting broke, their movements slowed. Elyra could see the cracks forming in their magic, the delicate balance they had maintained beginning to unravel. But as the balance shifted, she felt the cost of her actions pressing down on her. The magic she was using wasn't just fighting the shadow council. It was fighting the curse itself, pulling at the threads that held it together. And those threads were tied to Rhyven, to the land, to everything she had sought to protect.

Rhyven struck down one of the shadow council's leaders, their mask shattering as they fell. The remaining leaders retaliated with a surge of power, their voices rising in desperation. But Elyra didn't stop. She pressed forward, the staff's light growing brighter until it was almost blinding.

And then it happened.

The staff pulsed one final time, the light expanding outward in a brilliant wave. The shadow council's leaders cried out as the light consumed them, their forms disintegrating into nothingness. The storm above began to break, the clouds parting to reveal a faint glimmer of sunlight. The battlefield fell silent, the rebels retreating in confusion and fear.

Elyra collapsed to her knees, the staff clattering to the ground beside her. Her chest heaved as she gasped for breath, her body trembling from the strain of the magic she had unleashed. Rhyven was at her side in an instant, his hands steadying her as she swayed.

"It's over," he said, his voice filled with relief and something else—something gentler.

She looked up at him, her vision blurry. "Not yet," she whispered. "The curse…"

Rhyven frowned, his hand tightening on her shoulder. "You broke it. I saw them fall. The curse is gone."

"No," she said, her voice trembling. "It's not gone. It's just… changed."

He didn't understand. She could see it in his eyes. And maybe that was for the best. The truth was too heavy to share, the choice she had made too complex to explain. She had altered the curse, shifted its balance, but it still remained. It had to. The kingdom needed it, needed its stabilizing force. But now, it was bound to her as well. She had taken on part of the burden, a piece of the darkness, so that Rhyven could remain whole.

She reached up, her hand brushing his cheek. "You don't have to carry it alone anymore," she said softly.

His expression softened, and for the first time, she saw the weight of everything he had endured begin to lift. The storm had passed, the battle was over, and for this brief moment, they stood together, unbroken.

Whatever came next, whatever the curse demanded in the future, they would face it together. Because their bond was stronger than fate, stronger than the curse. It was a love that had rewritten destiny itself.

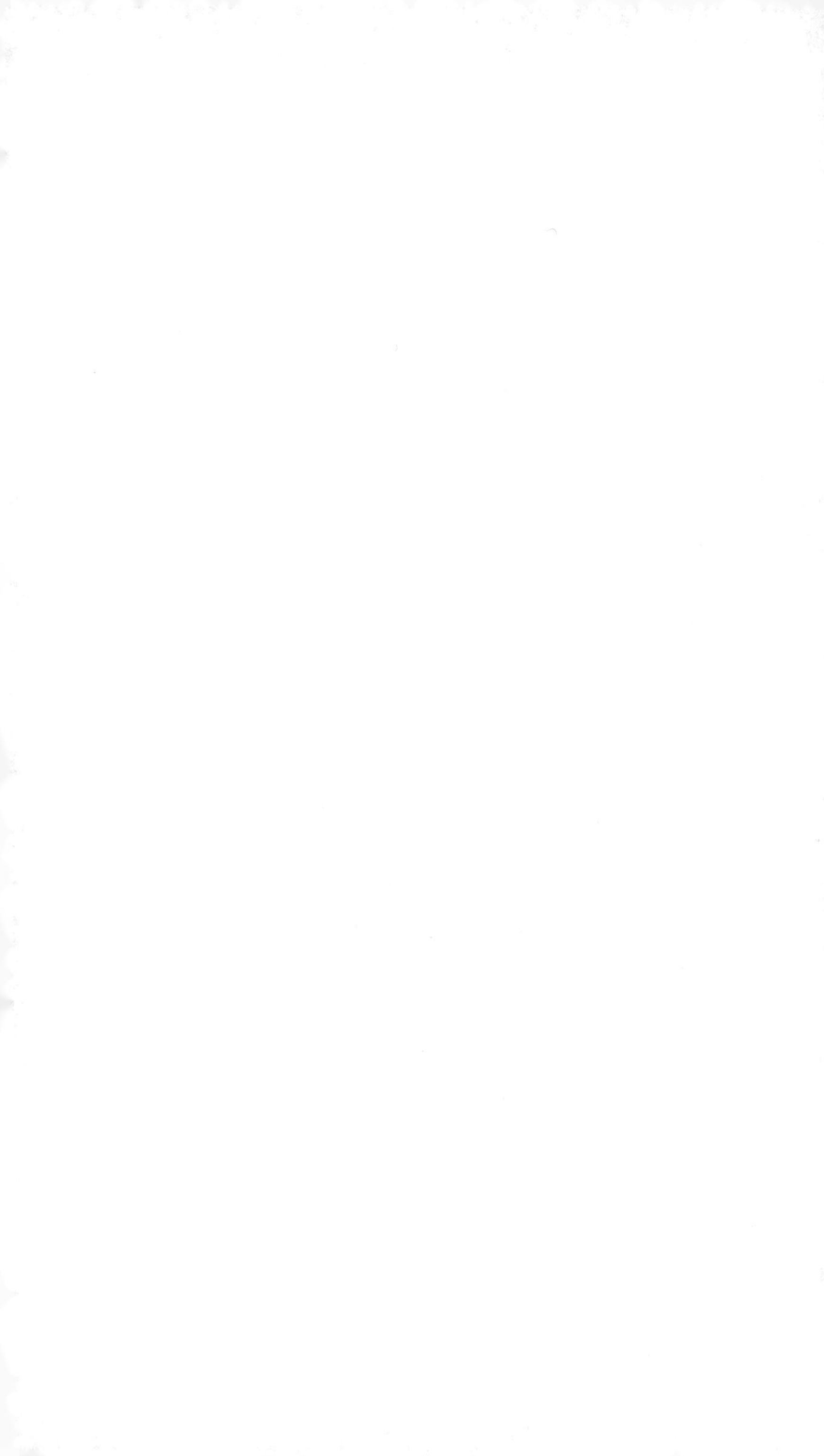

www.ingramcontent.com/pod-product-compliance
Lightning Source LLC
LaVergne TN
LVHW050635200726
843506LV00010B/1254